INTERPRETING TEXTS

'A brilliant series – an absolute gift for teachers! This superb series clarifies terminology and implicit meanings which to many students seem foreign. The books' methods and tactics are enjoyable and workable for both students and teachers, and the clear, evaluative and reflective models will enable students to obtain the necessary reflection in their own written responses.'

Kesner Ridge, Hagley Roman Catholic High School, Worcestershire, and Outstanding New Teacher 2002 (*The Guardian Teaching Awards*)

'This is the series we've all been waiting for! Tightly focused on the assessment objectives, these books provide an excellent aid to classroom teaching and self-study. Whether your school changes board or text, or decides to offer Literature and/or Language to 6th formers these books are still the tool that can make a real difference to results.'

Emmeline McChleery, Aylesford School, Warwick

Routledge A Level English Guides equip AS and A2 Level students with the skills they need to explore, evaluate and enjoy English. What has – until now – been lacking for the revised English A Levels is a set of textbooks that equip students with the concepts, skills and knowledge they need to succeed in light of the way the exams are actually working. The *Routledge A Level English Guides* series fills this critical gap.

Books in the series are built around the various skills specified in the assessment objectives (AOs) for all AS and A2 Level English courses, and take into account how these AOs are being interpreted by the exam boards. Focusing on the AOs most relevant to their topic, the books help students to develop their knowledge and abilities through analysis of lively texts and contemporary data. Each book in the series covers a different area of language and literary study, and offers accessible **explanations, examples, exercises, summaries, suggested answers** and a **glossary of key terms**.

The series helps students to learn what is required of them and develop skills accordingly, while ensuring that English remains an exciting subject that students enjoy studying. The books are also an essential resource for teachers trying to create lessons that balance the demands of the exam boards with the more general skills and knowledge students need for the critical appreciation of English Language and Literature.

ROUTLEDGE A LEVEL ENGLISH GUIDES

About the series editor

Adrian Beard was Head of English at Gosforth High School, Newcastle upon Tyne. He now works at the University of Newcastle Upon Tyne and is a Chief Examiner for AS and A2 Level English Literature. He is co-series editor of the Routledge Intertext series, and his publications include *Texts and Contexts*, *The Language of Politics* and *The Language of Sport* (all for Routledge).

TITLES IN THE SERIES

The Language of Literature
Adrian Beard

How Texts Work
Adrian Beard

Language and Social Contexts
Amanda Coultas

Writing for Assessment
Angela Goddard

Original Writing
Sue Morkane

Comparing Texts
Nicola Onyett

Transforming Texts
Shaun O'Toole

Texts through History
Adele Wills

Interpreting Texts
Kim Ballard

INTERPRETING TEXTS

Kim Ballard

Routledge
Taylor & Francis Group

LONDON AND NEW YORK

First published 2005
by Routledge
2 Park Square, Milton Park, Abingdon, Oxon OX14 4RN

Simultaneously published in the USA and Canada
by Routledge
270 Madison Ave, New York, NY 10016

Routledge is an imprint of the Taylor & Francis Group

© 2005 Kim Ballard

Typeset in Galliard by Keystroke, Jacaranda Lodge, Wolverhampton
Printed and bound in Great Britain by TJ International Ltd,
Padstow, Cornwall

British Library Cataloguing in Publication Data
A catalogue record for this book is available from the British Library

Library of Congress Cataloging in Publication Data
Ballard, Kim
  Interpreting texts / Kim Ballard.
    p. cm. — (Routledge A level English guides)
  1. Discourse analysis. I. Title. II. Series. Includes index.
  P302.B297 2005
  401′.41—dc22

                                            2004027820

ISBN 0–415–33436–5 (hbk)
ISBN 0–415–33437–3 (pbk)

CONTENTS

PREFACE

This book deals with a process which is central to the study of all English subjects at A Level, namely the interpretation of texts. It deals with both spoken and written texts, and with non-literary and literary varieties. It aims to develop both skills for interpretation and the knowledge needed for exploring texts on various levels and using different approaches. It also explores how and why different readers will form different interpretations of the same text. The wide-ranging approach begins by looking at texts as compilations of words and sentences and finishes by looking at them in socio-historical and cultural contexts.

Each chapter contains a number of exercises. When the exercise introduces a new idea, there will usually be suggestions for answers immediately following. When the exercise checks to see if a point has been understood, or if some of the information about the text needs to be withheld, suggestions for answers are given at the back of the book.

Words defined in the Glossary on pp. 81–6 are given in bold when used for the first time, or when reintroduced at a significant point.

ASSESSMENT OBJECTIVES

The AS/A2 specifications in English are governed by assessment objectives (or AOs) which break down each of the subjects into component parts and skills. These assessment objectives have been used to create the different modules which together form a sort of jigsaw puzzle. Different objectives are highlighted in different modules, but at the end of AS and again at the end of A2 each of the objectives has been given a roughly equal weighting.

The ideas and activities in this book will relate to the following assessment objectives. The ones which are most central have been italicized:

English Language

AO1: You must communicate clearly the knowledge, understanding and insight appropriate to the study of language, using appropriate terminology and accurate and coherent written expression.

AO3: You must know and use key features of frameworks for the systematic study of spoken and written English.

AO4: You must show that you can understand, discuss and explore concepts and issues relating to language in use.

AO5: You must show that you can distinguish, describe and interpret variation in the meanings and forms of spoken language according to context.

English Literature

AO1: You must communicate clearly the knowledge, understanding and insight appropriate to literary study, using appropriate terminology and accurate and coherent written expression.

AO3: You must show detailed understanding of the ways in which writers' choices of form, structure and language shape meanings.

AO4: You must articulate independent opinions and judgements, informed by different interpretations of literary texts by other readers.

AO5: You must show understanding of the contexts in which literary texts are written and understood.

English Language and Literature

AO1: You must communicate clearly the knowledge, understanding and insights gained from the combined study of literary and linguistic study, using appropriate terminology and accurate written expression.

AO2: In responding to literary and non-literary texts, you must distinguish, describe and interpret variation in meaning and form.

AO4: You must show understanding of the ways contextual variation and choices of form, style and vocabulary shape the meanings of texts.

AO5: You must identify and consider the ways attitudes and values are created and conveyed in speech and writing.

ACKNOWLEDGEMENTS

The author would like to thank the following copyright holders:

Extract from *Winnie-the-Pooh* by A. A. Milne copyright under the Berne Convention, reproduced by permission of Curtis Brown Ltd., London.

'Adlestrop' by Edward Thomas reproduced by kind permission of Myfanwy Thomas.

Extract from *I Don't Know How She Does It* by Allison Pearson published by Chatto & Windus used by permission of The Random House Group Limited.

Extracts from *The Waste Land* by T. S. Eliot reproduced by permission of Faber & Faber Ltd.

Extracts from 'Love Songs in Age' by Philip Larkin published by Faber & Faber Ltd and Farrar Strauss & Giroux.

Gervais/Merchant for permission to use a scene from *The Office* by Ricky Gervais and Stephen Merchant.

Professor Jon Stallworthy for kind permission to use his edition of 'Dulce et Decorum Est' by Wilfred Owen from *The War Poems* (Chatto & Windus, 1994).

Extracts from ITN coverage of the D-Day commemorations on 6 June 2004 reproduced by permission of ITV News.

Extract from the *Sun*, Monday 7 June 2004, reproduced by permission of the *Sun*/NI Syndication.

The author would also like to thank the following students:

Freddie Byrne, Christina Cole, Georgina Day, Helen Doran, Ed Latham, Miranda Lee and Julia Tubman.

INTRODUCTION

CHAPTER 1

Interpreting texts is essentially what A Level studies in English are all about. Whether you are studying language, literature or both, the central activity in which you will be involved is looking at examples of speech and writing with the purpose of arriving at a fuller understanding and appreciation of their meaning. The primary purpose of this book on interpreting texts is to explore how a range of approaches can be used to establish those meanings, and how a text can disclose different meanings depending on the reader or the context.

When we refer to a **text** in English studies, we mean any stretch of speech or writing which can be regarded as a complete unit. A text is typically made up of any number of sentences, although a sign that simply states 'no smoking' is a text. By contrast, a 200,000-word novel is also a text. When studying texts at A Level, it is inevitable that you will sometimes be looking at extracts and sometimes at complete texts.

When students begin an A/AS Level course in English, they are often under the impression that there is only one 'correct' way in which to interpret any text they are studying. Whereas it is true to say that some texts are unlikely to provoke very much disagreement as to what exactly they mean, the accepted view is that there is no definitive interpretation of any text. Although it would clearly be inappropriate to offer maverick interpretations of a text simply to make this point, there is no reason not to accept different interpretations as valid, provided they are informed and logically argued. Literary texts in particular lend themselves to multiple interpretations and there are, theoretically, as many interpretations as there are readers.

Interpretation of all spoken and written texts, whether non-literary or literary (and the division between these is increasingly being seen as debatable or artificial anyway), is a complex process, often surprisingly so. Much of the time, our encounters with texts don't seem to place any great demands on us. For example, a chat with a friend in the college canteen doesn't usually leave us scratching our heads trying to 'interpret' what has gone on. However, there are as many processes operating in an everyday conversation as there are involved in teasing out the meanings of a poem you may be studying for your course. It's simply that we are so used to interpreting some kinds of texts that we barely notice we're doing so, while other types of text require more conscious effort. The chief purpose of this first chapter is to consider the complexity which interpretation of texts involves, and to identify the different **levels** on which interpretation occurs. Each subsequent chapter then explores these levels in more detail.

A 'SIMPLE' EXAMPLE

To begin thinking about what 'interpreting' means and to begin to appreciate the complexity of this process, we will start with what appears to be a very simple text:

> *three pints today please*

Quite possibly, your first reaction to seeing this text is that it doesn't need interpreting at all. In other words, its purpose and meaning are transparent: it's a note (probably left by a resident in an empty milk bottle outside their house) for the milkman to deliver three pints of milk when he receives the request. (For the purpose of this discussion, we will assume the resident is female and the milkman is male.) It's a very short text consisting of only four words: does it really need 'interpreting'?

Let's begin by considering the milkman for whom the note was actually intended. It's certain he would have had no difficulty in identifying what the resident wanted, and he would subconsciously have made a number of deductions which are not explicit in the text. His full interpretation of the resident's note would have been something like: 'I, a resident of this household, would like you, the milkman, on receipt of this note, to leave three pint-sized containers filled with pasteurized cow's milk somewhere near this building, and I am assuming this will be on the same day as I am making the note available to you.' In other words, when the milkman saw 'three pints today' his interpretation was that

- It was a request for a particular service he offered
- Three pints of milk (not beer) were wanted
- A particular type of milk (cow's not goat's, and pasteurized) was wanted
- He should leave the bottles or cartons of milk near the house
- He should leave them on the same day as he received the note

Not only this, but the milkman may also have made other (subconscious) deductions from the note. The use of the **politeness marker** 'please' would suggest that the resident was appreciative of his services. In addition, the **noun phrase** 'three pints' and the **adverb** 'today' together carry the implication that three pints was not the normal quantity, with the resident typically having one or two pints of milk delivered. (If they normally had four pints, the likelihood is that they would have written '*only* three pints today please'.) Finally, although the note is referred to above as a 'request', the milkman may well have viewed it as a demand, given the resident's expectation that he was obliged to deliver the milk. This shows that the intention behind the creation of a text is also open to interpretation.

Clearly, the milkman, who is the **addressee** or **recipient** of the text, was actually doing rather more interpreting than you might initially have assumed. What, however, about the resident who wrote the note? What choices did she make in composing the note, given its very specific purpose? Initially she chose to use simple, everyday words, because these were appropriate for an unremarkable everyday event. She knew the milkman would be able to interpret the full meaning of 'three pints today' and so she was able to use **ellipsis**. It would have been absurd for the resident to have written the 'full' version of the note given above. She also wanted to show that the note was a request for a service which she appreciated (not a demand she expected to be fulfilled), hence the use of 'please', as already discussed. Perhaps most significantly, she knew how to format the note – not as a letter, or a memo or news bulletin – but using the simplicity and brevity typical of notes of this kind. In fact, she chose a 'note to the milkman' **schema**: she adopted a form used by thousands of other people throughout the country every day – and it wouldn't have occurred to her to write the note in any other format.

In terms of the temporal (or time) context in which the note was written, the resident knew that the milkman would be the interpreter of 'today' at the point of receiving the note. She may in fact have written the note the night before, in which case she was really wanting the milk 'tomorrow', but of course she was thinking ahead to the point in time when the milkman would read the note and how he would interpret 'today'. In other words, she was aware (probably subconsciously) of the **deictic** properties of some words – the way their meanings shift according to aspects such as time and place.

This brings us (again) to the social context in which the text was written. As 'outsiders' studying the note, we made the initial assumption that it was indeed written by a resident for a milkman and the topic was milk. However, imagine the note in a different context, such as a garden centre, where the same words might refer to the amount of water an assistant should give to each of the saplings in the greenhouse. This shows that the social context in which a text is created and received is often relevant to its meaning.

On a historical note, imagine, in a hundred years' time, visiting a social history exhibition presenting life at the beginning of the twenty-first century. In the hall devoted to food, one of the exhibits is a milk float (now an obsolete vehicle) and a display of the various goods which milkmen used to deliver, as well as some examples of bills and other texts, including the very note we have just been discussing! One visitor remarks to another how this note is a good example of the patronizing attitudes of householders of the time towards tradesmen and represented a classist expectation (thankfully now disappeared) that some people were born to provide menial services for others which they were perfectly capable of performing for themselves. Now that absolutely everyone bought their milk from a supermarket (and this was increasingly becoming the case at the time the note was written) the bourgeoisie struggle to maintain dominance over the working class was over.

WHAT THIS EXAMPLE SHOWS

The discussion of the note to the milkman is designed to show you how interpretation of texts is a complex process. As well as considering both the author and the recipient of the note and their respective roles in composing and interpreting it, we have also looked at the conventions involved in constructing a text, the temporal and social context in which the text was written and received, and possible interpretations of the text by observers not involved in its original production but able to take a long view of its meaning. The result of these considerations is that we now have a much fuller interpretation of the text's 'meaning', with this understanding functioning on a number of different levels. The fuller exploration of these levels is the purpose of this textbook, and the subsequent chapters will take you through them step by step.

Exercise 1

Look at the following example, this time a literary text. Read it carefully and then answer the questions concerning your interpretation of the text that follow.

Bermondsey

It aint like your regular sort of day.

   Bernie pulls me a pint and puts it in front of me. He looks at me, puzzled, with his loose, doggy face but he can tell I don't want no chit-chat. That's why I'm here, five minutes after opening, for a little silent pow-wow with a pint glass. He can see the black tie, though it's four days since the funeral. I hand him a fiver and he takes it to the till and brings back my change. He puts the coins, extra gently, eyeing me, on the bar beside my pint.

---

1. The extract is written in the **first person** (I/me). What picture did you form of this 'speaker' or **persona**, and why?
2. Did you think the persona and the author were the same person? Why/why not?
3. Who did you think the persona was addressing – you the reader or some implied addressee who is also a character in the novel?
4. What deductions did you make about the time and place in which this scene occurs?
5. What type of literary work did you think this was from? Did you form any thoughts about where in the text the extract occurred?
6. Although this is only a very short extract, did you form any initial impressions about any social or political standpoint existing in the novel?

Suggestions for answer

Your first impression was probably that the speaker is a working-class character, and the clue to this is in the use of two **non-standard grammatical features** – 'aint' and '*don't* want *no* chit-chat'. If you know that Bermondsey is a place in East London, then you may well have assumed the speaker was from this area, hence these **dialect** features. You also probably identified the speaker as male (he is a white male, and his name is Ray), not just because he is wearing a tie but because of the traditional associations of working-class men with pubs and beer-drinking.

It is unlikely that you thought the persona and author were the same person. There are two reasons for this. One is that in **first person narratives** the storyteller is conventionally a fictitious character constructed by the author and who has a specific role in the story. The other reason is the cultural (although not entirely accurate) assumption that novelists are most typically users of **Standard English** while this speaker has a non-standard dialect.

It is quite difficult to establish who the character Ray is addressing. Clearly, he can't be addressing you as a real person, as he inhabits a fictitious world in which you have no existence. You may have noticed that the extract is written in the **present tense** (Bernie *pulls* me a pint, That*'s* why I*'m* here) which creates the impression that the scene is unfolding as Ray speaks. It's like a commentary of what is taking place at the bar. Clearly, the addressee is not also at the bar, as what would be the point of describing what they can see for themselves? The paradox is that Ray is addressing no one, and only by opening the novel and starting to read do we even bring the character to life. However, as readers we do develop some sense that Ray is speaking to us. The informal use of the **second person** 'your' in the opening sentence creates this feeling, as too does the explanation of Ray's thought processes in 'That's why I'm here', which is a contrast to the description which makes up most of the rest of the extract.

The scene is a pub in Bermondsey. The author is relying on the reader having **shared cultural knowledge** about pubs in order to understand what is going on. Ray never actually states that it's a pub, but the second sentence (Bernie pulls me a pint) indicates this is the likely venue, as the pub is the place where pints are pulled. In the 'note to the milkman' example above, we discussed the assumption that 'pint' referred to milk. Here the clue to 'pint' referring to beer is in the **collocation** 'pull a pint'. The expression 'to pull a pint' is used in the context of pouring beer, but never in the context of other liquids such as milk, blood or water. Other lexical items such as 'five minutes after opening', 'pint glass', 'till' and 'bar' reinforce our interpretation that the setting is a pub as they all belong to the **semantic field** of public houses.

If we know about pub opening-times, we will probably deduce that the time of day is late morning. This is supported by Ray's comment that this isn't a 'regular sort of day', which suggests we're going to hear about the events of the day. The period itself is vaguely contemporary, as implied by 'fiver', and we are told a funeral has taken place four days earlier. (This is clearly setting up an expectation that we are going to learn more about this funeral, and we also may wish to know why Ray is still, or once more, wearing a black tie. In fact, he has arranged to meet some friends in the pub, and they are setting off to Margate to scatter the ashes of the deceased man, Jack Dodds, in the sea.)

As already mentioned, the extract is from a novel. The main clue to this is of course the construction of the character Ray and the narrative signals, namely the mention of the day which, not being 'regular', implies a story worth telling, and then the sequential recounting of events, particularly the pint being pulled, the money being paid and the change being given. However, the extract has some features in common with recounting a story face to face to a friend.

The extract occurs at the very beginning of the novel. The opening sentence, as discussed above, suggests the opening of a story. Without this, however, the extract could easily have occurred later in the narrative, with the funeral perhaps at the beginning.

The use of a non-standard dialect by the character of Ray and the fact of his being a regular at his local in Bermondsey (traditionally a working-class area) suggests Ray is a working-class figure. In other words, a member of the working class is being presented by the author as a first-person narrator. This gives Ray status as a key character in the novel, and the reader may therefore conclude that this author (like some other modern authors) is breaking from a tradition in English literature which positions members of the middle or upper classes as the main characters in novels.

A final point worth mentioning about this novel, *Last Orders*, relates to a criticism which was made of it when it was first published, a criticism which raises some interesting issues about the relationship of one text to another. *Last Orders* has a similar storyline to William Faulkner's 1930 novel *As I Lay Dying*. In Faulkner's story, the mother of a hapless and dysfunctional American working-class family dies, having expressed a wish to be buried with 'her people' in Jefferson, some distance away. The narrative is centred on the many difficulties the family encounter in taking her coffin by wagon to its final resting place. The construction of the novel is also similar to *Last Orders* in that it is told by a variety of characters. (Ray in *Last Orders* actually shares the narrative with some of his friends and with Jack's widow.)

Graham Swift came in for a lot of criticism on the grounds that he had **plagiarized** *As I Lay Dying* when writing *Last Orders*. In other words, the idea was not original, with Swift 'stealing' both the storyline and the structure from an earlier novel. However, in defence of Swift's work, which is an enjoyable novel in its own right, an awareness of what it owes to *As I Lay Dying* actually enhances the reader's enjoyment of *Last Orders*, and adds a new layer to their interpretation of the latter.

SUMMARY

This chapter has shown that the interpretation of a text:

- is a complex process, often surprisingly so
- needs to pay close attention to language features and language conventions
- needs to consider the originator (writer or speaker) of the text
- needs to take social and other external factors into account
- may be influenced by the political or theoretical standpoint of its interpreters, who are not necessarily the original recipients of the text
- may involve recourse to another text or texts
- may vary from audience to audience, but more than one interpretation may be valid

WORDS AND SENTENCES   CHAPTER 2

In Chapter 1 we saw that the process of interpreting a text is a complex one that involves thinking about language in a variety of ways, some relating mainly to the text itself, others to the circumstances in which the text was written. In this chapter we are going to take a closer look at how we interpret the words and sentences which make up texts and the **lexical** and **syntactic** choices which speakers and writers make when constructing texts.

WORD MEANINGS

Content words and function words

When we interpret the meanings of texts we tend to pay more attention to some words than others. For example, look at the following sentence, which is a description of *Shadow of a Doubt*, a 1943 film by Alfred Hitchcock, from *The Virgin International Encyclopedia of Film*:

> One of his most <u>disturbing</u> <u>films</u>, *<u>Shadow</u>* <u>was</u> <u>nominally</u> the <u>story</u> of a <u>young</u> <u>woman</u> who <u>learns</u> that a <u>favorite</u> <u>uncle</u> <u>is</u> a <u>murderer</u>, but at <u>heart</u> it <u>is</u> a <u>sobering</u> <u>look</u> at the <u>dark</u> <u>underpinnings</u> of <u>American</u> <u>middle-class</u> <u>life</u>.

The underlined words are the ones which carry the essential meaning of the sentence. It would be possible to grasp much of this meaning if the other words were omitted. For example, if we take just one section of the sentence we get: '*Shadow* was nominally . . . story . . . young woman . . . learns . . . favorite uncle is . . . murderer'. By contrast, without the underlined words, the other words in the sentence seem fairly meaningless: 'One of his most . . . the . . . of a . . . who . . . that a . . . a . . . but at . . . it . . . a . . . at the . . . of . . .' The underlined words, which carry precise meaning, are known as **content words**, and this large group of words is made up of **nouns**, **adjectives**, **verbs** and **adverbs**:

nouns   films, *Shadow*, story, woman, uncle, murderer, heart, look, under-pinnings, life

adjectives	disturbing, young, favorite, sobering, dark, American, middle-class
verbs	was, learns, is
adverbs	nominally

There are thousands of content words in a language, but, by contrast, only a very small number of the little words like 'that' and 'of', which are known as **function words**. (Function words include **pronouns**, **determiners**, **prepositions**, **conjunctions** and **auxiliary verbs**.)

When we hear or read a text, most of the time we concentrate our attention on the content words because they carry the essential meaning. When we speak spontaneously or read aloud, we give relatively little stress to function words. (Try to read aloud the sentence about *Shadow of a Doubt* placing the emphasis on the function words rather than the underlined content words. This doesn't come naturally!) Sometimes, however, when interpreting texts, it's important to pay attention to function words as they often carry significant pieces of information.

Exercise 1

Two of the most commonly used determiners in English are the **definite article** 'the' and the **indefinite article** 'a/an'. We use these hundreds of times every day to make distinctions between specific and unspecified events, people and objects:

> Did the uncle commit *the* murder?
> Did the uncle commit *a* murder?

For illustration, think about some of the titles of Hitchcock's movies:

Group 1   *The Lodger*
          The Trouble With Harry
          The Birds
          The House Across the Bay

Group 2   *Strangers on a Train*
          To Catch a Thief
          Dial M for Murder

---

1. The titles in Group 1 are all noun phrases which begin with the determiner 'the'. What effect does the presence of this function word have?
2. *The House Across the Bay* contains the preposition 'across'. How would the effect of the title differ with the prepositions 'by' or 'on'?
3. In Group 2, how would the meaning of the first two examples differ if the determiner 'a' were replaced by 'the'?
4. What would happen if *Dial M for Murder* became *Dial M for A Murder*?

Suggestions for answer

If you are familiar with the work of Alfred Hitchcock, then you may well have assumed that all these films are thrillers or horror films, and this will possibly have coloured your interpretation of the titles. In all these examples, the effect of the determiner 'the' suggests that the film will focus on specifics – a particular lodger, a particular group of birds and a particular house. *The Trouble With Harry* suggests that Harry has one particular fault or characteristic which is going to get him into trouble or cause trouble for others. *The Birds* suggests a specific group of birds. Arguably, this title sounds sinister because of the implication that the birds themselves might be aware of belonging to a specific group.

The use of the preposition 'across' in *The House Across the Bay* obviously suggests the location of the house. 'The house' implies it is the only dwelling, and its relative inaccessibility (by being across the bay) may well indicate a desirable place of retreat. On the other hand, the hint of remoteness and isolation may mean that something sinister could happen at the house.

Strangers on 'a train' rather than 'the train' implies that the specific train itself is irrelevant. What will be significant in the film is the people and the fact of them being on a train journey rather than, say, a car journey. The title *To Catch a Thief* suggests that a theft will take place but that the identity of the thief will be unknown, not just to the other characters in the film, but also to the audience.

Dial M for Murder suggests that just a phone call will take you into a whole world of death and homicide, something far more threatening and sinister than one isolated murder.

The meanings of content words

We have seen from the previous exercise that sometimes it is useful to focus on function words as they are often giving us important information. Most of the time, however, we draw our interpretation of a text from the content words, which carry the bulk of the meaning. In longer stretches of text, content words do not operate in isolation but work together to build up impressions and ideas. In this section, we will be looking at several aspects of the meanings of content words.

Polysemy

> A snake goes into a bar and asks for a pint. The barman says, 'I'm sorry, I can't serve you', and the snake says, 'Is that because I'm a snake?' And the barman replies, 'No, it's because you can't hold your drink'.

This simple joke is constructed on the basis of **polysemy** – when a word or expression has more than one meaning. Here, the joke is playing on the two meanings of being able to 'hold your drink'. Many of the content words in English are polysemous. (We touched on this point in Chapter 1.) You only need to browse through a dictionary to see just how common polysemy is. Most of the time we have no difficulty in identifying the relevant meaning of a word because the context in which it is used guides us towards this, but often writers or speakers will deliberately make use of the multiple meanings of words (or the similar sounds of separate words through puns and plays on words).

Exercise 2

Here is a list of some of the situations and varieties in which speakers and writers might deliberately play upon the multiple meanings of words:

- jokes
- advertisements
- crosswords
- poetry
- speeches
- names of shops

1. Collect some examples of some or all of these types, adding further examples of your own if you can.
2. Identify the word or expression which is polysemous, and consider which meanings are being brought into play in the context in which the example occurs.

There are no suggestions for answer to this exercise.

Avoiding ambiguity

Although, as we have just seen, many words in English are polysemous and – more to the point – the multiple meanings are being deliberately exploited by the speaker or writer, there are also many occasions when it is important to avoid any **ambiguity** in what you say or write. In other words, the listener or reader should not be left in any doubt about what you mean. For instance, a lawyer drawing up a contract will be paid to make sure that the wording of that contract is as clear and unambiguous as possible since legal difficulties could arise if they fail to achieve this. In everyday life, we often assume that language use is unambiguous, but this is not everyone's perception. This is cleverly illustrated by Mark Haddon in his 2003 novel *The Curious Incident of the Dog in the Night-Time*. The narrator of the story is a fifteen-year-old autistic boy called Christopher who is hoping to find out who killed his neighbour's dog, Wellington, and he explains how the simplest public sign can be confusing for him:

I decided that I was going to find out who killed Wellington even though Father had told me to stay out of other people's business.

This is because I do not always do what I am told.

And this is because when people tell you what to do it is usually confusing and does not make sense.

For example, people often say 'Be quiet,' but they don't tell you how long to be quiet for. Or you see a sign which says **KEEP OFF THE GRASS** but it should say **KEEP OFF THE GRASS AROUND THIS SIGN** or **KEEP OFF ALL THE GRASS IN THIS PARK** because there is lots of grass you are allowed to walk on.

Synonyms and near synonyms

We have just seen that many content words have multiple meanings, and this can be exploited by speakers or writers for various effects. By contrast, there are many words in English which have similar meanings to other words, largely because the word-store or **lexicon** of English is much larger than that of most other languages. The reason for this is a historical one: over the centuries English – which is essentially a Germanic language – has absorbed thousands of words derived from many other languages, particularly French and Latin. This has resulted in there being many words that are very close in meaning. Words that are identical or extremely close in meaning are **synonyms**, but many linguists believe there are few, if any, true synonyms in English (since why would you need two words of identical meaning?). However, there are many near-synonyms.

Exercise 3

The following extracts are taken from the novel *Crime and Punishment* by the Russian writer Fyodor Dostoevsky. It was written in the 1860s. The story concerns a young and impoverished student, Rodion Raskolnikov, who murders an old woman from whom he has borrowed money. At first, he believes her life is valueless and that he is justified in killing her in order to steal money and jewellery on which he can live. This section describes Raskolnikov's behaviour some hours after he has committed the murder.

As you will see, the extract is given in two different translations. Translators into English have an interesting challenge in that the extensive lexicon of English in comparison to other languages means that a translator may often have more than one word to choose from. This means that there are likely to be significant differences between translations.

1. Look at the pairs of words which have been underlined and consider the differences in meaning between the words in each pair. (You may wish to go on and select some further paired examples for consideration.) Use a dictionary to compare meanings and, if possible, compare your responses to someone else's.

2. What does this exercise reveal about the process of translating from one language to another, or equally the process of updating an older text by preparing a modern version?

David Magarshack's 1966 translation	David McDuff's 1991 translation
1 He rushed to the window.	He rushed to the window.
2 There was enough light, and he began to examine himself <u>hurriedly</u>, from head to foot, all his clothes; were there any <u>traces</u> left?	There was quite a lot of light now, and he <u>quickly</u> began to examine himself all over, from head to toe, all his clothes, to see if there were any <u>marks</u>.
3 But it was impossible to do it just like that: shivering, he began taking off all his clothes and again examined them thoroughly.	But he could not do it like that: shaking with ague, he began to take off all his things and examine them thoroughly.
4 He <u>turned everything inside out</u>, to the last thread, to the last rag, and unable to trust himself, repeated the examination three times.	He <u>ransacked everything</u>, everything, right down to the last thread, the last scrap of cloth and, lacking confidence in himself, repeated the examination some three times.
5 But there seemed to be nothing; no trace at all; only where the hem of his trousers was worn did the frayed edges show thick traces of <u>congealed</u> blood.	But it was all right, there seemed not to be any marks; only his trouser-ends, in the place where they hung down and rubbed the ground, retained some thick traces of <u>coagulated</u> blood.
6 He <u>seized</u> his large penknife and cut off the frayed edges.	He <u>grabbed hold of</u> his large folding knife and pared the rubbed ends.
7 There seemed to be nothing more.	There seemed not to be anything else that required attention.
8 Suddenly he remembered that the purse and the <u>articles</u> he had taken out of the old woman's trunk were still in his pockets.	Suddenly he remembered that the purse and the <u>objects</u> he had stolen from the old woman's chest were all of them still in his pockets, and had been there all this time!

9 Till then it had never occurred to him to take them out and hide them!	It had taken him until now to think of removing them and hiding them away!
10 He had not even thought about them when he was examining his clothes!	He had not even remembered about them just then, as he had been examining his clothes!
11 What was the matter with him?	What was wrong with him?

Suggestions for answer

In Sentence 2, 'hurriedly' has a stronger sense of panicking and urgency than 'quickly', while 'traces' has a suggestion of providing clues. In Sentence 4, 'ransacked' sounds rather more chaotic and desperate than 'turned everything inside out' which, while still having a hint of desperation, suggests a more methodical approach. In Sentence 5, 'congealed' is commonly collocated with blood and has connotations of an accident or attack, while 'coagulated' sounds more scientific and therefore less emotive. In Sentence 6, 'seized' possibly sounds more sudden and determined than 'grabbed hold of'. Finally, in Sentence 8, 'articles' implies Raskolnikov was more aware of what the specific items were than 'objects'.

What the exercise shows is that anything we read in translation is one person's intrepretation of the original text and as such may well give a different impression of the original from that of another translator. Similarly, if we look at modernized versions of English texts, such as the poetry of Chaucer or the Bible, we are only looking at one possible version of the original, not a definitive one.

SENTENCE MEANINGS

As speakers and writers of English, we not only make lexical choices, but also syntactic ones. In other words, we have choices about the way in which we construct sentences and order sentence elements. In addition, the construction of a sentence is also part of its meaning.

To illustrate this, look at the two translations of a further extract from *Crime and Punishment*, this time from near the end of the novel, when Raskolnikov has been imprisoned for his crime:

David Magarshack's 1966 translation

Siberia. On the banks of a broad, deserted river stands a town, one of the administrative centres of Russia; in the town there is a fortress; in the fortress there is a prison. In the prison Rodion Raskolnikov, convict of the second class, has been confined for nine months. Almost eighteen months had elapsed since the crime was committed.

David McDuff's 1991 translation

Siberia. On the bank of a wide, lonely river there is a town, one of Russia's administrative centres; in the town there is a fortress, in the fortress a prison. In the prison there is a penal exile of the second category, Rodion Raskolnikov. Since the day he committed his crime almost one and a half years have passed.

Both versions begin with the **minor sentence**: 'Siberia'. This single noun focuses the reader immediately and abruptly on the change of location. The next two sentences are structured in such a way that they move us from a larger to a more specific location and finally to Raskolnikov: river – town – fortress – prison – convict/exile. The final sentences in each version contain the same information but in reverse order:

	Focus of first part of sentence	Focus of second part of sentence
David Magarshack's 1966 translation	**TIME PASSING** 'Almost eighteen months had elapsed . . .'	**THE CRIME** '. . . since the crime was committed'.
David McDuff's 1991 translation	**THE CRIME** 'Since the day he committed his crime . . .'	**TIME PASSING** '. . . almost one and a half years have passed'.

The effect of this is that the 1966 translation, by positioning the time information at the start of the sentence gives that more prominence, while the 1991 version gives more prominence to the committing of the crime which resulted in the imprisonment.

Agency

Another difference you may have noticed between the two sentences above is that the **clause** 'since the crime was committed' makes no mention of Raskolnikov as the perpetrator of the crime, whereas 'since the day <u>he</u> committed his crime' includes reference to Raskolnikov as the **agent** of the crime. By arranging a sentence as **passive** rather than **active** it is possible to avoid indicating agency, although this can be included optionally:

Active sentence (having agent as **subject**) 'Raskolnikov committed the crime'.
Passive sentence (no indication of agent) 'The crime was committed'.
Passive sentence (with agent indicated in a *by*-**phrase**) 'The crime was committed by Raskolnikov'.

The choice between active and passive constructions is one strategy for subtly changing the meaning of a sentence. On a factual level, these two sentences have the same meaning:

'Raskolnikov committed the crime'
'The crime was committed by Raskolnikov'

In terms of how we interpret the sentences, however, there is a subtle difference between them, with the first giving more attention to the murderer, and the second giving more attention to the crime.

Exercise 4

Here are some further sentences where the agent has not been included. For each sentence, consider why the agent has not been included in terms of the meaning of the sentence.

Suggestions for the answer can be found at the back of the book on p. 77.

	Source	Sentence
1	*The Times*, 2 June 2004	A SCHOOLBOY has been praised after using his initiative to rescue a friend who was floundering in heavy seas.
2	Leaflet trying to raise money for the crisis in Sudan in 2004	So far an estimated 1.2 million people have been displaced, and many of these people are trapped in compounds which have become little more than concentration camps.

3 Bill Bryson in his 2003 work *A Short History of Nearly Everything*, describing the start of the universe. (Look at the underlined sentences.)

<u>In three minutes, 98 per cent of all the matter there is or will ever be has been produced.</u> We have a universe. It is a place of the most wondrous and gratifying possibility, and beautiful, too. <u>And it was all done in about the time it takes to make a sandwich.</u>

SUMMARY

In this chapter we have seen that:

- we pay most attention to content words, but function words are also important
- content words are often polysemous, and this can be exploited by speakers and writers
- English is rich in words whose meanings are virtually synonymous but subtly different
- the way in which sentences are constructed is part of their meaning

DISCOURSE

In Chapter 2 we were looking at texts in some detail by focusing on the meanings of individual words and also by considering how the way sentences are structured is part of their meaning. In this chapter, we move on to consider the larger units made up by sentences, namely texts or **discourse**.

When we talk about a text or a piece of discourse, we are normally referring to a stretch of speech or writing that we regard as being a complete unit. As we noted in Chapter 1, there is no upper limit on the length of a text. Equally, many of the texts we encounter in everyday life are as short as a sentence or even a word. For instance, notices such as 'No Entry' or 'Departures' are texts, as are proverbs such as 'Too many cooks spoil the broth'. Very long texts are likely to be written rather than spoken. One of the longest books in the English language, for example, is Vikram Seth's novel *A Suitable Boy* (1993). This runs to nearly 1350 pages in the Phoenix House hardback edition, a length of approximately 600,000 words.

COHESION AND TEXTUALITY

When we hear or read any text other than the very shortest types, we take it for granted that the sentences which make up the text belong together and in a particular order. Of course, in conversation or other types of spontaneous unplanned speech, it may be that a speaker makes errors in constructing the text. For example, when telling a humorous anecdote, a speaker might leave out an important detail at the beginning which they have to insert later. In general, however, speakers are remarkably efficient at structuring and organizing what they say.

Most texts that we encounter possess a level of **cohesion** that is sufficient to indicate the text is an orderly whole. Cohesion is the way in which the sentences in a text 'stick together'. ('Cohesion' comes from the Latin verb 'cohaerere' meaning 'to hold or cling together'.) We are so used to the fact that texts are cohesive that much of the time we barely notice cohesive devices at work.

Exercise 1

The following text is from A. A. Milne's 1926 children's classic, *Winnie-the-Pooh*. In this extract from Chapter 6 it is the birthday of Eeyore the donkey. Piglet has a balloon which he is planning to give Eeyore as a birthday present.

Read the extract carefully, and then answer the following questions:

1. Look at the underlined **clause** in line 1 and the underlined words in line 25. What is their function in terms of linking this extract to the section which has gone before, and in linking the sections of this extract?
2. The balloon is an important element in this extract. Identify all the words which refer to the balloon, either directly or indirectly. How do they give cohesion to the passage?
3. What do you notice about the style of this extract in terms of the level of difficulty, and how is this related to the audience for which the story was written, namely children?
4. Many adults are fans of *Winnie-the-Pooh*. In what ways do you think an adult reader might respond to this text differently from a child?

> <u>While all this was happening</u>, Piglet had gone back to his own house to get Eeyore's balloon. He held it very tightly against himself, so that it shouldn't blow away, and he ran as fast as he could so as to get to Eeyore before Pooh did; for he thought that he would like to be the first one
> 5 to give a present, just as if he had thought of it without being told by anybody. And running along, and thinking how pleased Eeyore would be, he didn't look where he was going . . . and suddenly he put his foot in a rabbit hole, and fell down flat on his face.
>   BANG!!!???***!!!
> 10 Piglet lay there, wondering what had happened. At first he thought that the whole world had blown up; and then he thought that perhaps only the Forest part of it had; and then he thought that perhaps only *he* had, and he was now alone in the moon or somewhere, and would never see Christopher Robin or Pooh or Eeyore again. And then he thought,
> 15 'Well, even if I'm in the moon, I needn't be face downward all the time,' so he got cautiously up and looked about him.
>   He was still in the forest!
>   'Well, that's funny,' he thought. 'I wonder what that bang was. I couldn't have made such a noise just falling down. And where's my
> 20 balloon? And what's that small piece of damp rag doing?'
>   It was the balloon!
>   'Oh, dear!' said Piglet. 'Oh, dear, oh, dearie, dearie, dear! Well, it's too late now. I can't go back, and I haven't another balloon, and perhaps Eeyore doesn't *like* balloons so *very* much.'

25   <u>So</u> he trotted on, rather sadly <u>now</u>, and down he came to the side of
      the stream where Eeyore was, and called out to him.
         'Good morning, Eeyore,' shouted Piglet.
         'Good morning, Little Piglet,' said Eeyore. 'If it *is* a good morning,'
      he said. 'Which I doubt,' said he. 'Not that it matters,' he said.
30   'Many happy returns of the day,' said Piglet, having now got closer.

Suggestions for answer

The **subordinate clause** in line 1 'While all this was happening' has the function
of a bridging device. 'All this' refers to what has previously been described (Pooh
has been getting his present ready for Eeyore), but the use of the **subordinating
conjunction** 'While . . .' indicates that our attention will now be directed to
something else that is going on. In line 23, the adverb 'so' indicates an outcome
and therefore provides a link between what has just happened (the balloon has
burst) and what Piglet decides to do next. The adverb 'now' later in the sentence
reinforces the current situation (namely that Piglet is sad because the balloon has
burst). Elements such as these adverbs and the subordinate clause at the beginning
are known as **discourse markers**. These perform the function of indicating the
starts and end sections of discourse. They are important because they help to guide
a reader or listener through the text.

The balloon is referred to in various ways. Here are the references, italicized:

line 2	Eeyore's *balloon*. He held *it* . . . , so that *it*
line 5	give *a present*
line 9	*BANG!!!???***!!!*
line 11	he thought that the whole world *had blown up*
line 18	I wonder what *that bang* was
line 20	And where's my *balloon*?
line 20	And what's *that small piece of damp rag* doing?
line 21	It was the *balloon*!
line 23	and I haven't another *balloon*
line 24	perhaps Eeyore doesn't like *balloons* so very much.

Inevitably, the noun 'balloon(s)' occurs several times. This kind of repetition
provides the passage with **lexical cohesion**. Since this is a children's story, 'balloon'
may occur more frequently than in a novel for adults, but this degree of repetition
would not be unusual in spontaneous speech. In line 2, the pronoun 'it' is used
twice to refer to the balloon without repeating the noun. This is an example of
anaphoric reference, when a pronoun refers back to a previously mentioned
element. **Anaphors** can provide cohesion both within sentences and across
sentence boundaries, as in line 2.

In line 5, the noun phrase 'a present' also refers to the balloon, as does the noun
phrase 'that small piece of damp rag', which describes the balloon after it has

exploded. The **onomatopoeic** 'BANG' in line 9 describes the bursting sound, as does the noun phrase 'that bang' in line 18. Piglet at first thinks that the world 'had blown up' and this verb, like the noun 'bang', is drawn from the semantic field of explosions. This provides further cohesive links with the balloon.

This extract is not particularly difficult since *Winnie-the-Pooh* is written primarily for children. The lexis is fairly simple, and most of it is concrete. Only the adverb 'cautiously' might be regarded as being more difficult. There is a high frequency of repetition in the extract, and this too is a signal that the text is directed at younger readers. Most texts sustain a consistent **register** in this way, and this is a further cohesive device. You may also have noticed that the extract is a **narrative**. It tells the story sequentially, which makes it easy to follow, and the simple past tense is used throughout, as is conventional.

An adult's initial understanding of the text may differ from a child's in that a child, like Piglet himself, may not at first realize that the explosion Piglet hears is actually the balloon bursting. Also, an adult would probably be more aware of the humour in the passage, created largely through Piglet's naivety. In addition, the characters in *Winnie-the-Pooh*, although animals, have human characteristics – for example, Eeyore's melancholy – and an adult might well see the story more as an exposition of human nature and of human friendships.

DRAFTS AND REVISIONS

Although there is normally a sense of completeness about many pieces of discourse, we need to be aware that often, beneath its fixed surface, there exists a fluidity to a text. It may well be that the 'finished' piece of discourse with which we are presented is an edited and adapted version of what was originally composed. This is particularly true of written discourse. For example, when we pick up a daily newspaper we do so with the expectation that what we will find within it is a collection of finished reports and articles. However, almost all the articles we read will have been revised and altered in some way by a subeditor. Very rarely are written texts composed and completed without any changes or revisions. Shakespeare's plays are a good example of textual fluidity. Most of the plays exist in more than one printed book, and one of the problems editors face is which version they should use.

In spoken language, texts can also be regarded as fluid. A key speech given in the House of Commons will have been written in advance; and in politics in particular the need for the careful weighing of words will almost undoubtedly lead to many changes to a draft before the speech is ready to be delivered. The former Prime Minister, Sir Winston Churchill, is said to have spent many hours and even days preparing some of his most important speeches. If speech is spontaneous (as it most typically is), then often it lacks that polished quality which we typically expect of written or scripted pieces. When we speak spontaneously, our speech is peppered with non-fluency features. These include items such as hesitations ('um', 'er', 'erm') and false starts which are perfectly natural when you are trying to think about what you want to say and to say it at the same time. Much of the time, we barely notice non-fluency features in other people's speech.

Some linguists and critics take the view that a text is never truly finished. This can be a useful concept to bear in mind. We have seen already that interpretation of texts involves processes which occur on different levels, and so the act of interpretation is of necessity a complex business. At the same time we should also be aware that a text may be subject to further alteration, or that it has already been revised in some way.

Exercise 2

Poets, for whom writing is an intricate craft, often spend a lot of time revising the drafts of their poems. In order to achieve an effective interplay of sound and meaning, every word needs to be just right. Many poets keep the original versions of their poems, and it can be interesting to compare the first draft with any interim versions and with the finished version.

Edward Thomas (1878–1917) wrote the following poem to capture the memory of an unanticipated event on a train journey in June 1914 when the train from London to Herefordshire made an unexpected stop at the country station of Adlestrop. This is the poem he wrote in January of the following year:

Adlestrop

Yes, I remember Adlestrop—
The name, because one afternoon
Of heat the express-train drew up there
Unwontedly. It was late June.

5 The steam hissed. Someone cleared his throat.
No one left and no one came
On the bare platform. What I saw
Was Adlestrop—only the name

And willows, willow-herb, and grass,
10 And meadowsweet, and haycocks dry,
No whit less still and lonely fair
Than the high cloudlets in the sky.

And for that moment a blackbird sang
Close by, and round him, mistier,
15 Farther and farther, all the birds
Of Oxfordshire and Gloucestershire.

The opening stanza of this poem gave Thomas some trouble, and he tried several versions before deciding on what you see above. Here are two earlier attempts at the first stanza:

Example 1	Example 2
Yes, I remember Adlestrop—	Yes, I remember Adlestrop—
At least the name. One afternoon	At least the name. One afternoon
Of heat the express train drew up there	Of heat the train slowed & drew up
Against its custom. It was June.	There unexpectedly. 'Twas June.

Compare these two earlier versions with the version on which Thomas finally decided, considering the ways in which your interpretation of each version varies. You may find it helpful to read the whole poem aloud before you begin. You should focus on:

1. changes to the relationship between the first two sentences in the drafts
2. changes in choice of vocabulary
3. changes to the final, simple sentence
4. the relationship between the different versions of the first stanza and the rest of the poem

Suggestions for answer

In the two drafts, the first two sentences are connected through the deictic adverb 'there' which in the second sentence refers back to Adlestrop. In the final version of the poem, the two sentences have been made into one using the conjunction 'because' to connect them. In other words, the specific reason why the poet remembers Adlestrop is now revealed as being due to the train stopping there. The opening reads as if the poet is answering a question (suggested by the use of 'yes') and wishes to explain his response.

The first change to the lexis of the poem is the omission of the adverbial 'at least' from the beginning of the second line. The loss of this phrase now gives the impression at the start of the poem that the only or central thing the poet remembers about the place is its name (which the poet would have seen on a sign on the station platform). However (and in answer to question 4), this impression changes as the poem develops. It is as if the poet's memory has been prompted by the mention of Adlestrop, and gradually more and more of the impressions of that day return to him.

The poet seems at first to have been uncertain whether or not to mention that the train was an express train. However, knowing that it is means we would not expect the train to stop at a small country station such as Adlestrop, and so this adds force to the notion that the break in the journey was unexpected. Two other possibilities for 'unwontedly' obviously occurred originally to the poet. 'Unwontedly' seems most effective largely because it is itself an unexpected word (less commonly used than 'against . . . custom' or 'unexpectedly'). Also, in the final version, 'unwont-edly' has been positioned at the start of a line and this gives it more prominence. The final lexical change is that the train, which in Example 2 'slowed & drew up', simply 'drew up' in the final version. The inclusion of 'express' would make the eight-syllable line too long if 'slowed' and 'drew up' were included, but in any case, it seems fairly obvious that a train would need to slow down before drawing up, so the omission of 'slowed' avoids the obvious and also adds to the simple economy of the language of this poem.

The decision to have 'It was late June' as the closing sentence of the first stanza again fulfils a practical purpose of achieving the required line length. However, and more significantly, it means that the stanza ends on two consecutive stressed syllables – 'late June'. Consequently, when the poem is being read aloud, the reader is forced to slow down at the end of the stanza, and this helps to enact the meaning of the train coming to a halt.

LITERAL AND FIGURATIVE LANGUAGE

One of the most important interpretative processes is establishing whether meaning is **literal** or **figurative**. Figurative language involves the use of comparisons such as **metaphors**, **metonyms**, **similes** and **personification**. Language is full of figurative meanings, not just in literary works but in everyday life.

When figurative language is used, its meaning can either work in conjunction with the literal meaning by developing and enhancing it, or the figurative meaning can introduce an element of surprise and cause the reader or listener to identify a new aspect to the literal meaning. For example, the following text, which is one of the film listings from the *Radio Times*, uses a conventional metaphor to describe the content of the film version of Jane Austen's novel, *Sense and Sensibility*:

> **Sense and Sensibility**
>
> *9.00 p.m.* Edward Ferrars's boyish charm eventually captures the more pragmatic Elinor Dashwood's heart.

The metaphor here is traditionally associated with romance, and uses the idea that a man can 'capture' a woman's heart in the way that an army captures a town or castle. Because we are familiar with this metaphor in our culture, it is unlikely to surprise us or challenge our expectations about a romantic story of this kind. By contrast, Craig Raine's 1979 poem 'The Butcher' describes how a butcher 'woos' his female customers with the meat he sells, for example, 'thin coiled coral necklaces of mince' or 'a leg of pork / like a nasty bouquet'. These images of courtship, unlike those in the *Radio Times* listing, are shocking because we hardly think of meat as romantic, and yet Raine's poem invites us to reconsider our view of what goes on in the butcher's shop.

Exercise 3

This exercise focuses on figurative language and is based on an extract from Allison Pearson's 2002 novel, *I Don't Know How She Does It*. It is the story of Kate Reddy, a successful city fund-manager who is trying to balance the demands of her job with bringing up two young children. In this scene, Kate and her family are getting ready for a long car journey to her in-laws' house for Christmas.

1. Identify some of the metaphors and similes in this extract which describe:
   - the children's toys and belongings
   - the children themselves
   - the car and its accessories

2. Comment on what these metaphors and similes contribute to the meaning of this extract, both in terms of description, and also its humour.

> 6.09 p.m.: Packing the car for the journey up North to my parents-in-law takes at least two hours. There is the first hour during which Richard pieces together a pleasing jigsaw of baby belongings in the boot. (Louis XIV travelled lighter than Ben.) Then comes the moment when he has
> 5   to find the key that unlocks the luggage box that sits like an upturned boat on our roof. 'Where did we put it, Kate?' After ten minutes of swearing and emptying every drawer in the house, Richard finds the key in the pocket of his jacket.
>   After Rich has told me to get the kids in the car 'right now', there
> 10   follows twenty minutes of frantic unloading as he 'just makes sure' he has packed the sterilizer which he 'knows for a fact' he wedged next to the spare tyre. This is followed by a furious re-packing, punctuated by 'fuck-its!', when items are squidged on top of one another any old how and the remnants are jammed into all available foot space front and back.
> 15   The Easi-wipe changing mat, the Easi-clip portable high-chair with its companion piece, the vermilion Easi-assemble portacot. Bibs, melamine Thomas the Tank Engine bowls. Sleepsuits. Emily's blankie – a tragic hank of yellow wool that looks as though it has been run over several times. We always travel with an entire bestiary of nocturnal comforters
> 20   – Ben's beloved Roo, a sheep, a hippopotamus in a tutu, a wombat that

is an eerie Roy Hattersley double. Ben's dummies (to be hidden from Richard's parents at all costs). Emily's surprise hamster is stashed in the boot.

25   Strapped into their seats in the back of the car like cosmonauts awaiting blast-off, Emily and Ben's contented bickering soon gives way to hand-to-hand combat. In a moment of weakness – when do I have a moment of strength? – I have opened the chocolate Santa dispenser meant for Christmas morning, and given them a couple of foil-wrapped pieces each to keep them quiet. As a result, Emily, who fifteen minutes

30 ago was wearing white pyjamas, now looks like a dalmatian with a dark brown muzzle around her mouth and cocoa smudges everywhere else.

   Richard, who has a heroic indifference to the cleanliness and general presentation of his offspring for eleven and a half months of the year, suddenly asks me why Ben and Emily look such a mess. What's his

35 mother going to think?

   I swipe at children with moist travel tissues. Three hours on the A1 lie ahead of us. Car is so overloaded it sways like a ship.

   'Are we still in England?' demands an incredulous voice from the back.

   'Yes.'

40   'Are we at Grandma's house yet?'

   'No.'

   'But I *want* to be at Grandma's house.'

   By Hatfield, both children are performing a fugue for scream and whimper. I crank up the *Carols from King's* tape and Rich and I sing

45 along gustily. (Rich is the descant specialist while I take the Jessye Norman part.) Near Peterborough, eighty miles out of London, a small nagging thought manages to wriggle its way clear from the compost heap that presently comprises the contents of my head.

   'Rich, you did remember to pack Roo?'

50   'I didn't know I was meant to be remembering Roo. I thought you were remembering Roo.'

Suggestions for answer

1. Here is a list of some of the examples you may have identified:

- The children's toys and belongings:
  '*a pleasing jigsaw* of baby belongings' (metaphor)
  '*an entire bestiary* of nocturnal comforters' (metaphor)
  'a wombat that is *an eerie Roy Hattersley double*' (metaphor)

- The children themselves:
  '*like cosmonauts awaiting blast-off*' (simile)
  '*like a Dalmatian with a dark brown muzzle*' (simile)
  'both children are performing *a fugue for scream and whimper*' (metaphor)

- The car and its accessories:
  'the luggage box which sits *like an upturned boat* on our roof' (simile)
  'Car is so overloaded it sways *like a ship*' (simile)

2. The metaphor of the baby belongings in the boot of the car is effective because 'jigsaw' suggests a children's toy. Also, Kate's husband, Richard, has spent time packing the boot very carefully, reminiscent of the way in which someone fits the irregular pieces of a jigsaw together neatly. The 'jigsaw' also provides an amusing contrast with what happens next when Richard has to unpack the boot to check for the sterilizer and when he then repacks, it's done 'any old how'.

The metaphor of the 'bestiary' is possibly less accessible that the 'jigsaw' example. It reflects the narrator's character as well educated. A bestiary is a medieval collection of descriptions and fables involving animals (or 'beasts', hence 'bestiary'). Bestiaries were serious, edifying texts and were often beautifully illustrated. Kate's choice of 'bestiary' to describe her children's animal toys is appropriate in that the children have a wide-ranging collection and the toys have about them something of the magical, unusual quality of the creatures in a bestiary. Kate mentions that the toys are 'nocturnal comforters' and so this toy bestiary also has a specific, positive purpose.

One of the toys, a wombat, reminds Kate of the politician Roy Hattersley. This metaphor of the wombat being his 'double' reminds us that the novel is written from the point of view of an adult and its humour appeals to an adult audience. The children themselves would not be able to draw this comparison.

The comparison of the children to cosmonauts is a way of suggesting that, for them, the car journey is something of an adventure. Like cosmonauts waiting for blast-off, the children have no control over the movement of the vehicle. The comparison to a space journey also perhaps reinforces the amount of time and trouble that has gone into the preparation for this journey, and how long the journey will seem to the children.

Emily has been eating chocolate and has got it round her mouth and over her white pyjamas, making her look like a 'dalmatian'. The comparison with a dog is appropriate for a child who is clearly fond of animals. The simile is extended by indicating that the chocolate around her mouth is like the dog's 'muzzle'.

After a while, the children start to 'scream and whimper'. Kate describes this mix of noises as a 'fugue'. A fugue is a piece of music in which the same tune is played in several parts, each starting at a different point. It is a term mainly associated with classical music, and again reflects Kate's education and interests. The unattractive noise of the children's 'fugue' is contrasted to the more pleasant sounds of the choir of King's College Cambridge singing Christmas carols.

The similes of the luggage box being 'like an upturned boat' and of the car swaying 'like a ship' both relate to sailing. As mentioned above, this journey has involved a lot of preparation, and there is a long distance to travel. The notion of sea travel helps to reinforce this, and again suggests that the journey is challenging and adventurous.

SUMMARY

In this chapter we have seen that:

- texts are normally cohesive, and various features contribute to their cohesiveness and textuality
- there is a fluidity to texts, even if they appear 'finished'
- meanings in texts can be either literal or figurative, and figurative meanings can work both with and against the text's literal meaning

---

INTERTEXTUALITY CHAPTER 4

So far, we have been looking at texts in some detail by concentrating on what goes on *within* a text. We have considered the meanings of individual words and of sentences, we have looked at figurative meanings, and we have also thought about links that exist within a text and that give it cohesion. In this chapter, we will move on to consider relationships between texts – what is known as **intertextuality** – and how our awareness of these relationships influences our understanding and appreciation of a particular text.

Intertextual knowledge helps us in our everyday encounters with a whole range of spoken and written texts. If our brains did not store intertextual knowledge, every encounter with a text would seem a new and alien experience! Perhaps more interestingly, an awareness of links between texts often shapes and changes a reader's or listener's interpretation of a text.

There are several types of intertextuality, but here they are presented for you in three broad categories:

1. quotation
2. content
3. genre

QUOTATION

Even in everyday speech, we are constantly using intertextuality, whether we are aware of it or not. For example, we have many expressions in contemporary English which are drawn from traditional sources such as the plays of Shakespeare or the King James Bible of 1611. Expressions such as 'to be cruel to be kind' and 'to wait with bated breath' are both drawn from Shakespeare, while 'keeping on the straight and narrow', and 'not suffering fools gladly' are drawn from the 1611 Bible.

The likelihood is that most speakers, if they use these phrases, are unaware of their original source. If speakers do become aware of the provenance of such phrases, then this probably enhances their understanding and appreciation of the language. Knowing about the links gives a sense of the tradition of English, and of the rich texture of the language. It reminds us of the importance many people place on our cultural heritage. However, remaining unaware of the connections does not mean we are less effective at using English.

Exercise 1

Advertisers and the media are particularly adept at exploiting intertextuality in order to make texts more memorable or striking. The expression 'bend it like Beckham' (referring to the England footballer, David Beckham, and his skill with the ball) has established itself as a text in contemporary culture. Speakers' awareness of this text was crystallized by the release of a film of that name in 2002. Since then, intertextual reference to the phrase has been made extensively in the media.

1. Look at the following newspaper headlines, and try to explain the nature of the intertextual references.

   (a) Bend it like Neville
        (*Daily Star*, 12 January 2003, referring to the player Gary Neville)
   (b) Will Beckham bend and accept move to Barcelona?
        (*New York Times*, 11 June 2003)
   (c) Splendid like Beckham
        (*Daily Mirror*, 18 April 2002)

2. Consider what you think the cultural significance of the phrase 'bend it like Beckham' has been. (You may wish to search the Internet for further intertextual examples.) Do you think it is as significant as phrases drawn from Shakespeare's plays, for example?

Suggestions for answer

'Bend it like Neville', (a), is a simple reworking of the phrase 'bend it like Beckham', with the substitution of Beckham's name with that of Gary Neville. The implication is that Neville is as skilful at bending the ball as Beckham himself. In 'Will Beckham bend and accept move to Barcelona?', (b), the headline is playing on the polysemous aspect of the verb 'bend'. It is still making reference to the collocation of 'Beckham' with 'bend', but instead of using the expected meaning of kicking the ball in a particular way, it's using the meaning of changing one's mind or giving in. 'Splendid like Beckham', (c), makes intertextual reference to the original phrase phonologically. 'Splendid' sounds similar to 'bend it' as the words almost rhyme, and the two-syllable shape is maintained too.

The phrase has been very influential in shaping people's awareness of David Beckham as a cultural icon, partly through the way it has encouraged comparison of others with him. In addition, it has provided journalists with a rich intertextual source, enabling the media to play a key role in developing a shared cultural consciousness through language. Arguably, an expression like this is more influential than the intertextual references to Shakespeare in contemporary English because speakers are more likely to be aware of its origin and therefore connect with the culture it represents.

CONTENT

Another way in which one text may be related to another is through its content and, particularly if it is a fictional text, through its story or narrative. In literature, writers often draw their inspiration from previous texts. For example, in Chapter 1 we noted that Graham Swift's 1996 novel *Last Orders* owed something to William Faulkner's 1930 novel *As I Lay Dying*. It is not that authors are 'stealing' from each other. Rather, writers recognize that they are working within a tradition or stream of writing and that it is almost impossible to create a text which is completely 'original'. Sometimes writers are paying tribute to texts which have had a formative influence on them. An example of this is Michael Cunningham's 1998 novel, *The Hours*, which pays tribute to Virginia Woolf's 1925 novel, *Mrs Dalloway*. In recent decades, many films have used literature as their source. For instance, Amy Heckerling's 1995 film *Clueless* is based on Jane Austen's novel *Emma* (first published in 1816), while Garry Marshall's 1990 romantic comedy *Pretty Woman* is described as 'a modern-day Cinderella fantasy'.

Exercise 2

Virginia Woolf's 1925 novel, *Mrs Dalloway*, as mentioned above, is the inspiration for Michael Cunningham's 1998 novel, *The Hours*. Even the title of this work is an intertextual reference, since Woolf's novel was originally to be called *The Hours*. *Mrs Dalloway* traces a day in the life of its eponymous central character, Clarissa Dalloway. In Cunningham's novel, there are three narrative strands tracing a day in the lives of three separate women. One of these is modelled very closely on Woolf's novel.

The extract below from *Mrs Dalloway* (set in London in 1923) is taken from quite near the beginning of the novel when Clarissa Dalloway, who is throwing a party that evening, has gone to Mulberry's the florist to get flowers. Miss Pym is assisting her when they hear a sudden explosion. In the extract from *The Hours* (set in New York at the end of the twentieth century), Clarissa Vaughan (the Clarissa Dalloway counterpart), is also throwing a party and has gone to buy flowers.

Begin by reading the extract from *The Hours* and *then* the extract from *Mrs Dalloway* which influenced it. How does your reading of *The Hours* shift or develop in the light of Woolf's novel?

The Hours

Clarissa chooses peonies and stargazer lilies, cream-colored roses, does
not want the hydrangeas (guilt, guilt, it looks like you never outgrew it),
and is considering irises (are irises somehow a little . . . outdated?) when
a huge shattering sound comes from the street outside.
5 "What was that?" Barbara says. She and Clarissa go to the window.
"I think it's the movie people."
"Probably. They've been filming out there all morning."
"Do you know what it is?"
"No," she says, and she turns away from the window with a certain
10 elderly rectitude, holding her armful of flowers just as the ghost of her
earlier self, a hundred years ago, would have turned from the rattle and
creak of a carriage passing by, full of perfectly dressed picnickers from a
distant city. Clarissa remains, looking out at the welter of trucks and
trailers. Suddenly the door to one of the trailers opens, and a famous
15 head emerges. It is a woman's head, quite a distance away, seen in profile,
like the head on a coin, and while Clarissa cannot immediately identify
her (Meryl Streep? Vanessa Redgrave?) she knows without question that
the woman is a movie star. She knows by her aura of regal assurance, and
by the eagerness with which one of the prop men speaks to her (inaudi-
20 bly to Clarissa) about the source of the noise. The woman's head quickly
withdraws, the door to the trailer closes again, but she leaves behind her
an unmistakable sense of watchful remonstrance, as if an angel had briefly
touched the surface of the world with one sandaled foot, asked if there
was any trouble and, being told all was well, had resumed her place in
25 the ether with skeptical gravity, having reminded the children of earth
that they are just barely trusted to manage their own business, and that
further carelessness will not go unremarked.

Mrs Dalloway

The violent explosion which made Mrs Dalloway jump and Miss Pym go
to the window and apologise came from a motor car which had drawn
to the side of the pavement precisely opposite Mulberry's shop window.
Passers-by, who, of course, stopped and stared, had just time to see a face
5 of the very greatest importance against the dove-grey upholstery, before
a male hand drew the blind and there was nothing to be seen except a
square of dove grey.

Yet rumours were at once in circulation from the middle of Bond Street
to Oxford Street on one side, to Atkinson's scent shop on the other,

10 passing invisibly, inaudibly, like a cloud, swift, veil-like upon hills, falling
    indeed with something of a cloud's sudden sobriety and stillness upon
    faces which a second before had been utterly disorderly. But now mystery
    had brushed them with her wing; they had heard the voice of authority;
    the spirit of religion was abroad with her eyes bandaged tight and her lips
15 gaping wide. But nobody knew whose face had been seen. Was it the
    Prince of Wales's, the Queen's, the Prime Minister's? Whose face was it?
    Nobody knew.

Suggestions for answer

Cunningham has updated the scene by making the mystery celebrity a movie
star rather than a member of the royal family or a senior politician. The famous
person is no longer in a motor car but in a movie trailer. Effectively, however, he
is reinforcing Woolf's point that people will always be interested in those who
are important or famous. (Cunningham's mention of the movie star's 'aura of
regal assurance' suggests that movie stars are treated as royalty in contemporary
American society.) Like Woolf, Cunningham shows that the presence of a celebrity
gives onlookers a feeling of awe, excitement and being watched over.

GENRE

Links between texts are established not just through quotations or through
content-based relationships, but also through the type of text, or **genre**. When we
encounter a text we often use our knowledge of the genre to which it belongs
to help us assimilate it. For example, many people read a national daily newspaper
and are therefore familiar with this particular genre, be it broadsheet or tabloid.
Once they have become familiar with the style and layout of their chosen
publication, they bring this intertextual knowledge to each day's edition. As far as
organization is concerned, for example, they will get to know where in the paper
the sections they are interested in appear, such as the sport section, or the letters
page or television listings. Long before this, they will have become used to the style
in which newspaper reports are written and will have learnt to skim the headlines
to help decide which reports they want to read. Similarly, readers get used to the
principle that the opening paragraph (known as the **lead paragraph**) of a newspaper report usually gives a summary of the key facts of the story followed by the
important details, with less central information towards the end of the report. This
expectation influences the way we read such reports as many readers stop reading
as soon as they feel they have discovered the key facts.

Although we rely on our knowledge of different genres to help us interpret the
texts we encounter throughout our everyday lives, it is important to remember that
a genre is not a fixed or rigid category: genres can change over time, and in any
one text, it may be possible to identify features drawn from more than one genre.

For example, Truman Capote's 1966 novel *In Cold Blood* draws on journalistic style for much of its effect. Authors will sometimes break the conventions of a genre in order to make their work distinctive or to foreground some aspect of it.

HUMOUR AND PARODY

Sometimes when textual conventions are broken the effect is a comic one, and sometimes speakers or writers break conventions in order to mock someone or something in the real world, or in another text. This is known as **parody**.

Exercise 3

The following extract is the opening of a fairy tale, 'The Princess and the Pea' that has been rewritten by James Finn Garner for a collection of 'politically correct bedtime stories'.

1. Identify the ways in which the author is parodying the traditional fairy tale genre. Does the parody change your view of fairy tales in any way?
2. Identify anything else which you think the author is parodying, and try to explain how.

The Princess and the Pea

In a kingdom over the hills and far away, there lived a young prince who was very full of himself. He was healthy, relatively handsome, and had had more than his fair share of happiness and comfort growing up. Yet he felt that he deserved something more. It was not enough for him
5   to have been born into a life of parasitical leisure and to keep the masses firmly under the heel of his calfskin boot. He was also determined to perpetuate this undemocratic tyranny by marrying only a real, authentic, card-carrying princess.

His mother the queen encouraged her son's obsession, despite the
10   obvious risks of hemophiliac or microcephalic grandchildren. Many years earlier, after a period of inadequate wellness, his father the king had achieved corporal terminality. This lack of a strong male presence gnawed at the prince on a subconscious level, and no amount of weekend retreats and male bonding with other young dukes and barons could relieve this
15   anxiety. His mother, for her own codependent and Oedipal reasons, did not bother to change or correct his selfish notions of unattainable perfection in a spousal lifemate.

In his quest for the perfect partner, the prince travelled far and wide, looking for someone to enslave in matrimony . . .

Suggestions for answer

Although the author is using the traditional ingredients of a fairy tale such as a distant land, a bachelor prince and a search for a princess, he is mocking these conventions by exposing the way in which fairy tales promote notions of privilege and social hierarchy as well as traditional male/female roles where the male makes the choice of partner, and where the young female is expected to be a model of perfection. Many children have grown up with a knowledge of traditional fairy tales, and it may well be that these politically correct versions, which are aimed at adults, would make the reader take a more critical view of the principles on which many fairy tales are based. (Another writer who has taken the fairy tale genre and subverted it is Angela Carter in her collection of short stories *The Bloody Chamber.*)

As well as parodying the traditional fairy story, the author is also parodying political correctness both by exposing some of the questionable values of fairy tales and by his mocking use of politically correct language. For example, he writes about the King's illness and death using **euphemisms** ('inadequate wellness' and 'corporal terminality') which are too excessive to be taken seriously. In addition, it could be argued that the author is mocking the tradition of psychoanalysis which explains people's behaviour in terms of parental influence, presenting the Prince's anxieties as the result of his father's death and questioning the nature of the Queen's feelings towards her son. The unexpectedness of this kind of analysis in what is conventionally a children's genre adds further to its mocking tone.

AN INTERTEXTUAL NETWORK

As we have already seen, intertextuality functions in a number of ways. In literature, it may be as simple as one author briefly quoting another, or it may be a question of revealing links and connections on a much larger scale. One of the pleasures of reading extensively (particularly reading literature) is derived from establishing links between texts. From this point, the reader ceases to read texts in isolation, but is instead able to construct a mental network of texts. With each new link that is established, the reader will be able to reconsider or develop their original interpretation of a text.

As an example of such an intertextual network, here is an apparently random set of texts from different periods:

Date	Title	Writer	Genre
from 1387	*The Canterbury Tales*	Geoffrey Chaucer	poetry
published 1902	*Heart of Darkness*	Joseph Conrad	short story
published 1922	*The Waste Land*	T. S. Eliot	poetry
published 1925	'The Hollow Men'	T. S. Eliot	poetry
released 1979	*Apocalypse Now*	John Milius and Francis Ford Coppola	screenplay

As you can see, this list ranges in time from the late fourteenth to the late twentieth century and includes two literary genres as well as a film screenplay. At first, it seems a rather disparate list, but there is an intricate web of connections between these texts.

A good point at which to begin our exploration of this web is with T. S. Eliot's 1922 poem, *The Waste Land*. This was a significant text of the 1920s as it aimed to explore the disintegration of European society after the First World War, focusing for much of the poem on the city of London. Aiming to reflect what he saw as the fragmentation and decay of culture in a post-war world, Eliot reflected this in the style of his poem. It is something of a jigsaw of images and is dense in intertextual references.

To begin with, we will look at the opening of *The Waste Land*, and compare it with the opening of Chaucer's 'Prologue' to *The Canterbury Tales*.

'Prologue' to *The Canterbury Tales*	'The Waste Land'
Whan that Aprille with his shoures sote	April is the cruellest month, breeding
The droghte of Marche hath perced to the rote,	Lilacs out of the dead land, mixing
And bathed every veyne in swich licour,	Memory and desire, stirring
Of which vertu engendred is the flour. . . .	Dull roots with spring rain.

Both extracts make reference to the month of April. Chaucer's prologue is a celebration of April as this is the month in which the rains bring life back to the earth and everything starts to grow again. A reader beginning *The Waste Land* who was familiar with Chaucer's prologue would therefore be especially struck by the contrastingly negative mood of Eliot's opening with its description of April as the 'cruellest' time of the year, despite the arrival of lilacs and spring rain.

Exercise 4

As mentioned above, *The Waste Land* is packed with intertextual references to other works, some of which Eliot identifies in his glossary, some not. Many of these works were older works, but one strikingly modern influence on *The Waste Land* was Joseph Conrad's 1902 short story *Heart of Darkness*. This describes a long journey upriver into the heart of a jungle in search of the enigmatic trader Mr Kurtz. The 'darkness' of the title refers not only to the depths of the jungle but also to the darkness to be discovered in oneself in such a place. Originally, T. S. Eliot took Kurtz's last words, 'The horror! The horror!' and used them as the epigraph to *The Waste Land*. (He later removed them but he chose a quotation from *Heart of Darkness* as the epigraph for his 1925 poem, 'The Hollow Men': 'Mistah Kurtz – he dead'.) However, the intertextual link is instead established through a passage in *The Waste Land* that echoes the opening of *Heart of Darkness*.

1. Study the two passages closely and identify the intertextual links here between 'The Waste Land' and *Heart of Darkness*.
2. What difference does it seem to have made that Conrad was writing in prose, while Eliot was composing poetry?

Heart of Darkness

The *Nellie*, a cruising yawl, swung to her anchor without a flutter of the sails, and was at rest. The flood had made, the wind was nearly calm, and being bound down the river, the only thing for it was to come to and wait for the turn of the tide.

The sea-reach of the Thames stretched before us like the beginning of an interminable waterway. In the offing the sea and sky were welded together without a joint, and in the luminous space the tanned sails of the barges drifting up with the tide seemed to stand still in red clusters of canvas sharply peaked, with gleams of varnished sprits. A haze rested on the low shores that ran out to sea in vanishing flatness. The air was dark above Gravesend, and farther back still seemed condensed into a mournful gloom, brooding motionless over the biggest, and the greatest town on earth.

> **The Waste Land**
>
> The river sweats
> Oil and tar
> The barges drift
> With the turning tide
> Red sails
> Wide
> To leeward, swing on the heavy spar.
> The barges wash
> Drifting logs
> Down Greenwich reach
> Past the Isle of Dogs.

Suggestions for answer

The river (the Thames) is central to both passages. Although Conrad's opening begins by focusing on the vessel, the *Nellie*, Eliot foregrounds the river by making it the subject of his first line. Eliot's river 'sweats / Oil and tar', and arguably this suggests something of the haze and the gloom mentioned by Conrad. The turning of the tide is also important in both passages as it gives a sense of change and expectation. There is a strong sense of location in Eliot's work, as in Conrad's, with Conrad referring both to the Thames and to Gravesend (where the *Nellie* is waiting), and Eliot describing how the logs drift 'Down Greenwich reach / Past the Isle of Dogs'. Like Conrad, Eliot also makes reference to the barges on the river and uses the verb 'drift' to describe their motion. He picks up on the 'red clusters of canvas' in Conrad's piece, converting this more simply to 'Red sails', and links them to 'the heavy spar' in line with Conrad's 'varnished sprits'.

Eliot's poetry is more impressionistic than Conrad's prose. He has selected just a few details, but a similar mood – the sense of expectancy and brooding – is established. In conventional narrative style, Conrad has written in the past tense, but Eliot uses present tense and this adds to the sense of a scene being painted. Some of the lines in the poetry are in regular iambic rhythm ('The river sweats', 'The barges drift', 'The barges wash') or something close to it ('With the turning tide', 'Past the Isle of Dogs'), and the rhythm of 'Oil and tar' is echoed by 'Drifting logs'. These echoing rhythms give a strangely hypnotic quality to Eliot's passage, and this is enhanced by the occasional and irregular use of rhyme (tar/spar, tide/Wide, logs/Dogs).

If you now look again at the list of works given above, you will see that Eliot's poems are followed by Francis Ford Coppola's 1979 film about Vietnam, *Apocalypse Now*. The central idea of *Apocalypse Now* is drawn from Conrad's *Heart of Darkness*, as in the film a US army officer, Captain Willard, is commissioned to travel deep into Cambodia in search of Colonel Kurtz, an officer who has set up a strange pagan community in the heart of the jungle over which he presides. Here, then, the intertextuality derives from the similarity of the central motif of both *Heart of Darkness* and *Apocalypse Now*, namely a river journey into dark territory. *Apocalypse Now* uses intertextuality in another way, by giving the character of Colonel Kurtz a fondness for the poetry of T. S. Eliot. One camera shot scans the books in Kurtz's room, and focuses on copies of *From Ritual to Romance* and *The Golden Bough*, both of which Eliot offers as references in his notes on *The Waste Land*. Towards the end of the film, not long before Kurtz's death, Kurtz reads to Willard from Eliot's 'The Hollow Men'. The screenplay of *Apocalypse Now*, therefore, not only draws ideas from Conrad and Eliot but also plays on the link between those two writers. The intertextuality allows the screenwriters to explore further aspects of colonialism and the psyche of Kurtz within the constraints of the film.

Exercise 5

We have seen that intertextuality can be more than a single passing reference of one text to another and can actually develop into a web of connections. As we become aware of these links, our understanding of the individual texts is deepened and enhanced. In addition, through intertextual links, we are able to see individual texts in a broader cultural context and thus gain a fuller appreciation of writers' concerns and preoccupations. Intertextuality does far more than just create links as it has the important function of developing the meaning of one text through its relationship with another.

Intertextual links such as those just outlined can only really be appreciated if you are familiar with the texts referred to.

1. If you have time, familiarize yourself with the key texts discussed above. You will probably find it easiest to read or watch them in order of composition: *Heart of Darkness*, then Eliot's poems, then *Apocalypse Now*. When you have read Eliot's poems, think how they are related in meaning to *Heart of Darkness*. Then, as you watch *Apocalypse Now*, consider how your understanding of these texts colours your reading of this film. Of course, you may find it interesting to watch the film first, and then watch it again when you have read the texts, so that you can see how your interpretation has developed.
2. Alternatively, see if you can identify a different intertextual network yourself, possibly using one of your set texts as a starting point.

There are no suggestions for answer for this exercise.

SUMMARY

In this chapter we have seen that:

- Intertextuality occurs in both everyday language and in literature.
- Intertextuality can take various forms.
- Knowledge of generic features helps us to assimilate texts.
- Intertextual references can connect seemingly unconnected texts and can develop into a network of connections.
- Intertextuality helps to establish a sense of culture and tradition, as well as explore ideas and establish meanings.

CONTEXT

In the previous chapter, we considered intertextuality: the relationships which texts have with each other and the different ways in which texts can be connected and intertextual links established. In this chapter, we will be considering not the relationships between texts, but the significance of the **context** in which a text is either produced or received.

By context, we mean the 'environment' of a text. However, there are many possible 'environments' in which texts can be produced, or can be heard or read. A consideration of the circumstances of a text's production or reception often plays a part in the way it is interpreted. For example, in studying a Victorian novel, we may interpret it in terms of when in the author's career it was written, or of the social climate in which it was written and how this might have influenced the content of the novel. These are interpretative considerations which are linked to the text's production. We could also consider different contexts of reception. For instance, we might look at the comments of critics who reviewed the novel when it was published and how critics' views have changed over time, leading on to a consideration of how a contemporary reader might interpret the novel. The interpretation of any text is dependent upon the receiver's knowledge of the world, and this is a further context. Often texts rely on our cultural knowledge for their interpretation, as we saw with the extract from *Last Orders* in Chapter 1.

CONTEXTS OF PRODUCTION

Situational contexts

A knowledge of the immediate situation in which a text is produced can often play an important part in its meaning. This is particularly true of informal, everyday conversation, where participants may make reference to their location or the activity in which they are engaged.

Exercise 1

This extract is from a conversation between two boys, Hugh and Leo, who are playing Warhammer. This is a fantasy war game which involves assembling and painting plastic figures before the battle can begin.

Which linguistic features of this conversation rely on situational knowledge to be fully understood?

Key

(.)	micropause
(26.0)	pause timed in seconds
(*inaudible*)	inaudible speech

	HUGH:	I'm actually going to adjust this guy really quite drastic
	LEO:	what are you going to do (.) no no (*inaudible*) (26.0)
	HUGH:	I'm gonna do him so he's like blowing the horn forward instead of out to the side
5	LEO:	oh yeah (21.0)
	HUGH:	sometimes I wish I could just settle for the basic kinda way but (1.0) hey (26.0)
	LEO:	(*inaudible*) fit together there (.) oh god they do that's amazing (11.0) how many do you need to have in this unit (.) is it ten
10	HUGH:	ten minimum (1.0) yeah probably best is about twenty or twenty-four (14.0)
	LEO:	(*inaudible*) (5.0) that's another four (2.0) are you gonna make a tank or a mortar (.) I mean a um
	HUGH:	cannon
15	LEO:	cannonball mortar
	HUGH:	I'm not sure yet (.) I think I might go for the cannon (4.0) I had to go for the other head because it was the only one that fit in the position (3.0)
	LEO:	it's good
20	HUGH:	yeah it's good (2.0) right where's the other arm (.) last arm (.) oh it's here (16.0)
	LEO:	right I'll do these (2.0) what are these things called
	HUGH:	handgunners

Suggestions for answer

It is possible for someone reading the transcription to get a reasonable idea of what is going on since there is sufficient vocabulary in the semantic fields of kit-making and of warfare to deduce what the boys are up to. However, the use of **deixis** reflects the dependence on knowledge of the situation for interpreting meaning. Hugh uses deictic words in line 1 ('*this* guy'), line 17 ('the *other* head'), and line

21 ('*here*'). Leo uses them in line 8 ('*they*'), line 9 ('*how many*', 'in *this* unit'), line 12 ('*another four*') and line 22 ('*these*' and '*these things*'). The boys would be able to work out the meanings of the deictic words because they could be holding or working on the figures or objects they refer to, or because they point at them.

In addition, there are long pauses in the conversation. These occur because the boys are involved in a practical activity which doesn't always require speech. During the pauses, they are getting on with assembling the figures. Leo's speech may be inaudible at times because he is effectively talking to himself.

Personal contexts

When considering the context in which a text is written or spoken, we may need to think about the individual who produced the text or the time in which they produced it – or both. Sometimes when we first encounter a text we are unaware of these factors, and when they come to light it may change our interpretation.

Sometimes we can approach a text with an awareness of its significance to the person who produced it. We often have access to information such as why the text was produced and the circumstances under which it was composed. In other words, the context of production is a transparent one. Consequently, we bring our knowledge about its production to our interpretation of the text.

Exercise 2

The following extract is the opening of a key speech given by the former Prime Minister, Margaret Thatcher, at the Lord Mayor's Banquet in London on 12 November 1990. Read the extract carefully and answer the following questions:

1. What clues can you identify in the speech that show that Thatcher is respectful of the context in which it is being given?
2. In line 6, Thatcher introduces a more personal note to her speech. What is your interpretation of the message she is trying to convey? What do you think may have prompted this message?
3. Thatcher uses a metaphor here based on cricket. What do you think the purpose and effect of this metaphor might have been?

> My Lord Mayor, My Late Lord Mayor, Your Grace, Your Excellencies, My Lords, Aldermen, Sheriffs, Ladies and Gentleman. May I begin by thanking you, My Lord Mayor, for your toast to Her Majesty's Ministers. May I thank you also for your splendid speech and congratulate you on
> 5 being elected Lord Mayor.
>
> Since I first went in to bat eleven years ago, the score at your end has ticked over nicely. You are now the 663rd Lord Mayor. At the Prime Minister's end, we are stuck on 49. I am still at the crease, though the bowling has been pretty hostile of late. And in case anyone doubted it,
> 10 can I assure you there will be no ducking the bouncers, no stonewalling, no playing for time. The bowling's going to get hit all round the ground. That is my style.
>
> May I also say a special word about His Grace the Archbishop of Canterbury . . .

Suggestions for answer

The opening of the speech uses the standard formula for a formal public occasion such as this. The guests at the speech are addressed using their honorific titles, and then thanks and congratulations are offered to the Lord Mayor, in whose honour the banquet is being given.

Thatcher begins by reminding her audience that she has been Prime Minister for a significant period of time ('I first went in to bat eleven years ago'). She seems keen to show she is tenacious and, like a batsman at cricket who wants to score lots of runs, she will not easily be removed from her position. In fact, at the time of giving the speech, Thatcher's leadership of the Conservative party was being challenged (hence her reference to recent 'hostile' bowling), and just over a fortnight later she was forced to resign.

The cricketing metaphor is appropriate as a batsman in cricket is up against the whole of the opposite team who are trying to get him out, so Thatcher was using the metaphor to show her determination. This metaphor uses humour at the beginning, and is cleverly developed. Her choice of a sporting metaphor may well have been influenced by the fact that the dignitaries at the banquet were predominantly male. (It has been observed that men are more likely to use metaphors drawn from sport than women are.) However, she may also have felt that her adoption of a 'male' metaphor would indicate that she was no less a force to be reckoned with simply because she was a female in a male-dominated political world. She would also have been aware that this speech would be televised and she could use it to reach a wider audience than the guests at the banquet.

Clearly, from the example just examined, some texts reveal their context of production fairly readily, and this guides us in our interpretation. Sometimes, however, the context in which a text was conceived or produced is not revealed to the audience. This can be particularly true of literary texts. When we read a poem or novel or watch a play or film we may well do so knowing nothing of the author's life in terms of what prompted them to produce the text or what personal concerns they were trying to address. Some critics argue that the author is no longer of concern once the text has been produced, as it is up to the reader to construct the meaning of the text without reference to the author's intentions. Nevertheless, it is often the case that we may reinterpret a text in the light of knowledge gained about the author's life.

Exercise 3

Look carefully at the following poem by Philip Larkin (1922–85). It describes a widow who finds some song books (music for voice and piano) that she has kept for many years.

1. When you have read it a few times, make a note of your interpretation of the poem. What is it saying about life and, particularly, about love?
2. Then turn to the 'Suggestions for answer' section at the back of the book and compare your interpretation to the one offered.
3. Then read the biographical details about the author and consider how this information causes you to rethink your original interpretation.

Love Songs in Age

She kept her songs, they took so little space,
   The covers pleased her:
One bleached from lying in a sunny place,
One marked in circles by a vase of water,
5 One mended, when a tidy fit had seized her,
   And coloured, by her daughter –
So they had waited, till in widowhood
She found them, looking for something else, and stood

Relearning how each frank submissive chord
10   Had ushered in
Word after sprawling hyphenated word,
And the unfailing sense of being young
Spread out like a spring-woken tree, wherein
   That hidden freshness sung,
15 That certainty of time laid up in store
As when she played them first. But, even more,

continued

> The glare of that much-mentioned brilliance, love,
>   Broke out, to show
> Its bright incipience sailing above,
> 20 Still promising to solve, and satisfy,
> And set unchangeably in order. So
>   To pile them back, to cry,
> Was hard, without lamely admitting how
> It had not done so then, and could not now.

Suggestions for the answer can be found at the back of the book on p. 77.

Social and historical contexts

A further consideration of context which might influence our interpretation of a text is the social or historical context in which it was produced. This can influence a text in various ways – in its style, its content and in the message it conveys.

Exercise 4

The following is an extract from a very long letter written at the end of the nineteenth century and published in 1905.

1. Read it carefully and then jot down a note of the impressions you form of

   - the writer
   - the person being addressed
   - the relationship between this person and the writer
   - the circumstances of the letter's composition

2. Then turn to the 'Suggestions for answers' section at the back of the book and find out the precise details of the context in which this letter was written.
3. Then consider to what extent the socio-historical context of the letter's composition is central to an accurate interpretation of the letter.

> The aim of love is to love: no more, and no less. You were my enemy: such an enemy as no man ever had. I had given you my life: and to gratify the lowest and most contemptible of all human passions, Hatred and Vanity and Greed, you had thrown it away. In less than three years you
> 5 had entirely ruined me from every point of view. For my own sake there was nothing for me to do but love you. I knew that if I allowed myself to hate you that in the dry desert of existence over which I had to travel, and am travelling still, every rock would lose its shadow, every palm tree

> be withered, every well of water proved poisoned at its source. Are you
> 10   beginning now to understand a little? Is your imagination awakening
> from the long lethargy in which it has lain? You know already what hate
> is. Is it beginning to dawn on you what love is and what is the nature of
> love? It is not too late for you to learn, though to teach it to you I may
> have had to go to a convict's cell.
> 15   After my terrible sentence, when the prison dress was on me, and
> the prison house closed, I sat amidst the ruins of my wonderful life,
> crushed by anguish, bewildered with terror, dazed through pain. But I
> would not hate you. Every day I said to myself: 'I must keep love in my
> heart to-day, else how shall I live through the day?' I reminded myself
> 20   that you meant no evil, to me at any rate: I set myself to think that you
> had but drawn a bow at a venture, and that the arrow had pierced a king
> between the joints of his harness. To have weighed you against the
> smallest of my sorrows, the meanest of my losses, would have been, I
> felt, unfair.

Suggestions for the answer can be found at the back of the book on p. 78.

CONTEXTS OF RECEPTION

So far we have looked at the personal and socio-historical circumstances in which texts are composed, and considered the effect of these circumstances on the texts themselves and our interpretation of them. In this section, we move on to look at how texts are received by readers and listeners, and how these contexts of reception may influence our understanding of a text.

When looking at the extract from *De Profundis* (Oscar Wilde's letter) in the previous section, you may have been surprised to learn of the circumstances in which it was written. If Wilde had lived in this age, he would not have found himself in prison. The modern reader approaches or 'receives' Wilde's text in a very different social context from the one in which it was originally written. In contrast to many of Wilde's Victorian contemporaries, most modern readers would feel a sense of outrage at Wilde's fate, both in terms of the reason for his imprisonment and the treatment he received in prison. In turn, this will influence their response to the letter.

Primary and secondary audiences

The extract from Wilde's letter also demonstrates a useful distinction which can be made between **primary** and **secondary audiences**. The person or persons for whom a text is originally or primarily intended is its primary audience. Therefore Lord Alfred Douglas was the primary audience for Wilde's letter. (It actually begins

'Dear Bosie'.) However, when Wilde was released from prison, he gave the manuscript to his literary executor, Robert Ross, with an instruction that it should be copied. In an earlier letter to Ross, he talked too about his name one day being cleared when the truth became known. This suggests that he realized his letter to Bosie would become public, and you may wish to consider how that might have influenced his writing of the letter. As readers who have access to the letter now, we belong to a secondary audience. We often need to think about different audiences when considering texts and need to be aware that the primary and secondary audiences may well have different responses to a text's meaning.

Exercise 5

Sometimes a writer will play upon the idea of different audiences for effect. Look at the following text, which is a scene from the second series of *The Office*, a satirical comedy written by Ricky Gervais and Stephen Merchant for the BBC. In this scene, David Brent, the office manager, a character desperate to be liked and respected, is conducting a staff appraisal with Dawn, the receptionist.

1. Within the dramatic context of a staff appraisal, how does Dawn respond to and interpret Brent's promptings?
2. How does the viewer interpret Brent's intentions differently from Dawn's? Why?

Scene 7. Int. Brent's office. Day

[*Brent is still in conversation with Dawn*]

BRENT: Okay, if you had to name a role model, someone who's influenced you, who would it be?

DAWN: What, like a historical person?

BRENT: No, someone in general life, just someone who's been an influence on you.

DAWN: I suppose my mum. She's just strong, calm in the face of adversity. Oh God, I remember when she had her hysterectomy—

BRENT: [interrupting]—if it wasn't your mother though. I mean, it doesn't even have to be a woman, it could be a—

DAWN: —a man?

BRENT: Yeah.

DAWN: Okay, well I suppose if it was a man, it would be my father—

BRENT: —not your father.

DAWN: No?

BRENT: Let's take your parents as read. I'm looking for someone in the, sort of, work-related arena whose influence—

DAWN: Right. Okay. Well, I suppose Tim then, he's always—

BRENT:	—well, he's a friend, isn't he? Not a friend. Someone in authority. Maybe—
DAWN:	Well then, I suppose Jennifer—
BRENT:	[annoyed] I thought we said not a woman, didn't we, or am I—
DAWN:	Okay, well, I suppose you're the only one who—
BRENT:	[mock-embarrassed] Oh. Embarrassing. That's backfired, hasn't it? Oh dear. Very flattering, but can we put me, I don't know . . .
DAWN:	Okay, Tim then.
BRENT:	[curt] We said not Tim, so, do you wanna put me or not?
DAWN:	Okay.
BRENT:	Right. So shall I put 'strong role model'?
DAWN:	Okay.
BRENT:	Yeah.

Suggestions for answer

Dawn takes the question of a role model very seriously as suggested by her asking whether it could be a historical person. When she then selects her mother, she has good reasons for doing so as she tries to explain. At the start of several turns, she says 'I suppose' and this suggests that, although she is taking the question seriously, no clear individual is emerging. When she is eventually led to propose Brent himself as her role model her unfinished remark 'I suppose you're the only one who—' implies she has been forced to eliminate all other possibilities, but that Brent had not instantly occurred to her as a possibility.

The audience realizes quite early on that Brent is leading Dawn to name him as her role model. He tries to narrow the field by suggesting it doesn't have to be a woman, and shouldn't be a parent or friend. His annoyance when Dawn suggests Jennifer and his mock-embarrassment when Dawn is forced to identify him as a role model confirm the audience's suspicions that this was what he wanted all along. At the end of the scene, he reveals his true intentions of making himself appear a good boss by suggesting he should be put down as a 'strong' role model.

NEW CONTEXTS, NEW MEANINGS

We have so far seen how various contextual factors can influence our interpretations of texts. A further point to consider is the way in which taking a text and placing it in a new context can significantly change its meaning.

Exercise 6

The following poem was written during the First World War by the poet Wilfred Owen, who fought on the western front and was killed there in 1918. Both the title of the poem and its closing lines make use of a quotation in Latin from the

Roman poet, Horace. 'Dulce et decorum est pro patria mori' means 'It is sweet and honourable to die for your country'. In Horace's original poem, it is used in the context of describing a virtuous young man who has trained for military service and is ready to do his duty. It was a quotation which was often used at the outbreak of the war.

Read the poem and consider how, by putting the quotation in a new context, Owen has changed its meaning.

'Dulce Et Decorum Est'

Bent double, like old beggars under sacks,
Knock-kneed, coughing like hags, we cursed through sludge,
Till on the haunting flares we turned our backs
And towards our distant rest began to trudge.
5 Men marched asleep. Many had lost their boots
But limped on, blood-shod. All went lame; all blind;
Drunk with fatigue; deaf even to the hoots
Of tired, outstripped Five-Nines that dropped behind.

Gas! GAS! Quick, boys! – An ecstasy of fumbling,
10 Fitting the clumsy helmets just in time;
But someone still was yelling out and stumbling,
And flound'ring like a man in fire or lime . . .
Dim, through the misty panes and thick green light,
As under a green sea, I saw him drowning.

15 In all my dreams, before my helpless sight,
He plunges at me, guttering, choking, drowning.

If in some smothering dreams you too could pace
Behind the wagon that we flung him in,
And watch the white eyes writhing in his face,
20 His hanging face, like a devil's sick of sin;
If you could hear, at every jolt, the blood
Come gargling from the froth-corrupted lungs,
Obscene as cancer, butter as the cud
Of vile, incurable sores on innocent tongues, –
25 My friend, you would not tell with such high zest
To children ardent for some desperate glory,
The old Lie: Dulce et decorum est
Pro patria mori.

Suggestions for answer

Owen has changed the meaning of Horace's original statement by exposing it as 'the old Lie'. He has effectively stated that the opposite of the original is true: that there is nothing sweet or honourable about dying for your country. On the contrary, the deaths of many soldiers during the battles of the First World War were horrific in terms of the physical suffering the men endured. This is brought home particularly forcibly by describing the death of one soldier in particular.

The poem begins with a description of a troop of soldiers leaving the front line for a rest period. Already, however, it is clear that they are in a dreadful physical state and therefore the adjectives of the title 'dulce' ('sweet') and 'decorum' ('honourable') seem to have little bearing on the content of the poem. As the soldiers march, they suddenly find themselves in a gas attack. The focus is then placed on one individual soldier who, unable to fit his gas mask in time, dies in the attack. Owen spares no detail of the soldier's death, describing vividly the terrible effects on his face and lungs as well as the indignity of the way the soldier was flung into the wagon. At the end of the poem, the poet addresses an implied listener and tells them (the original draft of the poem dedicates the poem to a female poet, Jessie Pope, who perpetrated the view that war was glorious) that, if they had seen what he has seen, they would realize that the much-quoted Latin tag is clearly a lie.

New meanings in non-literary contexts

One genre with which many modern listeners are familiar is the genre of song lyrics. In recent decades, rock, pop and jazz songs have been used in the soundtracks for films. Sometimes, the visual and cinematic context in which a song has been used has meant that a new interpretation has to be given to the words of the song. For example, Louis Armstrong's hit 'What a Wonderful World', composed by George Weiss and Bob Thiele in the 1960s, is a song which celebrates the beauty of the natural world as well as the delights of human love and friendship. (You can find the lyrics to this and any songs you use for Exercise 7 on the Internet.) When this song was first released in Britain in 1968, it was extremely popular for its feel-good factor. However, when the song was used in Barry Levinson's 1987 film *Good Morning, Vietnam* (set in Saigon in 1965, during the Vietnam war), it took on a far more sinister meaning. In this film, the song is played during a sequence which begins with positive images such as a beautiful dawn, children sleeping, and people working in the fields, but by the start of the second verse these are replaced by negative images such as bombs exploding in a village, soldiers arresting and executing young men in Saigon and violent street protests. In this context, the meaning of the song becomes ironic: the world depicted is far from 'wonderful'. It is likely, therefore, that a listener who had known this song when it was originally released and who then saw the way it is used in *Good Morning, Vietnam* to suggest a view of what took place, would remodel their interpretations of the lyrics in the light of that new context.

Exercise 7

Identify a selection of songs you know which have been used for film soundtracks and where the context of the film has resulted in you formulating a new interpretation of the lyrics. You may find it helpful to note your findings in a table with these headings:

1. title and date of song
2. my original interpretation of the song's meaning
3. film (date) and scene in which the song was used
4. how my interpretation of the lyrics changed in the context of the film

There are no suggestions for answers to this exercise.

SUMMARY

In this chapter we have seen that:

- An individual's personal circumstances may influence their production of a text.
- The historical and social context in which a text is produced may have been significant.
- An awareness of personal, social and historical contexts of production may influence the reader's or listener's interpretation of a text.
- A primary audience may interpret a text differently from a secondary audience.
- Texts can change their meanings when placed in new contexts.

REPRESENTATION

As we have already seen, the linguistic choices a speaker or writer makes (consciously or subconsciously) will affect the meaning of what they say or write, often in quite subtle ways. These choices may be related to lexical choices, sentence structures, what is included or left out of a text, and the amount of attention given to certain pieces of information. Because we are so familiar with our language and the different uses to which it is put, it is easy to be lulled into assuming that whatever is expressed about the world through language is, in some sense, 'real'. However, language itself is one step removed from reality. For example, nouns like 'car' or 'rain' or 'dog' are not those things themselves, but **representations** of them in speech or writing.

Not only are the individual words in a language representations of people, objects, places, events, and so on, in the world around us, but whole texts offer us representations of these things too. It is important to consider representation when we are interpreting texts because we often need to stand back and consider what version of reality a text is presenting to us. As we shall see, representation can influence the way we think about reality, and a comparison of how different texts represent the same person or idea can reveal significant differences in the way that person or idea is viewed.

Exercise 1

Below is a list of words and phrases which can be used in English to represent death. This is then followed by the poem 'In Flanders Fields' which was written by the Canadian poet John McCrae and was first published in 1915, the year after the First World War began.

1. Place the phrases in order of bluntness, starting with what you consider to be the most gentle. Jot down the associations or connotations of these phrases and when you think you might use them – if you would use them.
2. Look at how death is represented in McCrae's poem, which is written from the point of view of the dead soldiers. How gentle or blunt is his representation in relation to the items in the list?

- to die
- to snuff it
- to fall asleep
- to pass away
- to kick the bucket

In Flanders Fields

In Flanders fields the poppies blow
Between the crosses, row on row,
    That mark our place; and in the sky
    The larks, still bravely singing, fly
5 Scarce heard amid the guns below.

We are the dead. Short days ago
We lived, felt dawn, saw sunset glow,
    Loved and were loved, and now we lie
    In Flanders fields.

10 Take up our quarrel with the foe:
To you from failing hands we throw
    The torch; be yours to hold it high.
    If ye break faith with us who die
We shall not sleep, though poppies grow
15   In Flanders fields.

Suggestions for answer

Your list will probably have looked something like this:

> gentle: 'to fall asleep', 'to pass away'
> fairly neutral: 'to die'
> blunt: 'to snuff it', 'to kick the bucket'

You may have found it hard to decide between the two 'gentle' phrases. 'To fall asleep' is rarely used in speech but may be found in a context such as a book of remembrance or the announcement of a death in the newspaper. 'To pass away' is more commonly used in speech as a softer way of expressing 'to die'. Phrases such as 'to fall asleep' and 'to pass away', because they present the reality of death in a less direct way, are known as euphemisms. We often use euphemisms when we are trying to be tactful or respectful. By contrast, 'to snuff it' and 'to kick the bucket' are **dysphemisms**. In other words, they present reality in a harsh and sometimes painful way. It is unlikely we would use these terms to talk about someone we know who has died. We might, however, use them in the context of a joke or to talk about a fictitious event, such as a death in a film.

In John McCrae's poem, death is first introduced indirectly through the references to the crosses which mark the soldiers' graves. In the second stanza, the fairly neutral adjective 'dead' is used but there is something quite bald about the simple statement 'We are the dead'. The concept of being dead is then presented through contrast: only a few days before, the soldiers 'lived' and their living is heightened through the verbs 'felt', 'saw', 'loved', 'were loved'. Death is also represented using the euphemistic metaphor of sleep (a commonly used metaphor for death, both in literature and in other contexts). This idea is first introduced towards the end of the second stanza with the idea of the soldiers lying in Flanders fields. The notion of 'sleep' at the end is used in the context of the soldiers only being at peace in death if the living keep faith with them. (Unlike Owen's poem which we looked at in Chapter 5, death is here represented in a relatively gentle way and the horror of the soldiers' deaths is not referred to.)

REPRESENTING PEOPLE

If you asked several portrait painters or photographers to do a portrait of the same celebrity, you would expect each of them to portray that person in a different way according to their artistic style and their particular view of their subject. When speakers or writers represent people (themselves or others) through language, the same process occurs. No two representations are alike, although they may be similar.

There are many reasons why a writer or speaker might need to depict – or represent – an individual. For example, a novelist will need to introduce fictional characters, a historian will need to write about historical characters, and a current-affairs journalist will report on public figures such as politicians, chief executives, union leaders, and so on. Any representation of an individual or group of people, however factually accurate, is the result of the speaker's or writer's vision or view of that person.

Exercise 2

The following extracts are about the jazz singer Billie Holiday (1915–59) and are taken from two different books about jazz: *Jazz: A History of America's Music* by Geoffrey C. Ward and Ken Burns (2000) and *Jazz* by John Fordham (1993). Read the extracts carefully and then answer these questions:

1. What similarities can you identify in the way that Billie Holiday is represented in these extracts?
2. What differences can you identify, and how do you think these differences influence the impression you form of the singer? How might a reader rethink their reading of one of these texts when they subsequently read the other one?
3. Look at the language used to describe and present the scandals in the singer's life. How do these linguistic features influence your readings?

Extract 1: *Jazz* by John Fordham (1993)

In 1986, almost 27 years after her death and on what would have been
her 71st birthday, Billie Holiday had a star in her honour set into
Hollywood's Walk of Fame. Holiday, perhaps the only jazz vocalist
unequivocally regarded as a great jazz musician by the standards that
5   would be applied to instrumentalists like Louis Armstrong, Miles Davis
or Sonny Rollins, finally received mainstream acknowledgement for
achievements often obscured by scandal and sensationalism during her
lifetime. Because the mythology of Billie Holiday's strife-torn life fitted
so conveniently with the cliché of the self-abusive jazz genius, her
10   newsworthiness was more often based on stories of child prostitution,
drug dependency, stretches in jail, scandals, and a narcotics charge on her
deathbed. Even in her prime, meetings with the press both at home and
abroad would always involve fending off questions on these subjects, and
they rarely provided opportunities to talk about the music and musicians
15   she loved.

Extract 2: *Jazz: A History of America's Music* by Geoffrey C. Ward and Ken Burns (2000)

Billie Holiday had a tiny voice – barely a full octave. 'It just go up a little
bit and come down a little bit,' she once told an accompanist. 'This voice
of mine's a mess, a cat got to know what he's doing when he plays with
me.' And she chose to lead a life so full of self-abuse that it was a wonder
5   among her friends that she managed to survive even to the age of forty-
four. The sordid details of her private life, chronicled in lurid books and
twisted into soap opera by Hollywood, have too often been allowed to
obscure the fact that somehow, out of it all, she managed to make an
unforgettable art; that she was, after Louis Armstrong, the greatest singer
10   in jazz history.

Suggestions for answer

Both extracts make Holiday's status as a singer very clear. Extract 1 refers to her as
a 'great jazz musician' and Extract 2 offers the opinion that, after Armstrong, she
was 'the greatest singer in jazz history'. Both extracts use comparisons with other
performers (Louis Armstrong, incidentally, was both a vocalist and instrumentalist)
to enhance Holiday's reputation. Both extracts also give considerable attention to
aspects of her life other than her singing and mention how her private life attracted
a lot of media attention.

Extract 1 arguably elevates Holiday more than Extract 2 in that it begins with the mention of the pavement star in her honour in Hollywood. It also refers to the 'mythology' of Holiday's life, suggesting her legendary status. By contrast, Extract 2 reveals the person more by mentioning the 'tiny voice' (which suggests a degree of vulnerability) and by using quotations from Holiday herself. Therefore, a reader who referenced both these texts would need to consider and reconsider Holiday as both a private individual and as an icon.

Although both extracts make it clear that Holiday was an outstanding jazz singer, and seemingly criticize those who were more interested in her private life, the way Holiday's private life is presented may provoke the reader's curiosity. Both extracts use very emotive language when talking about it: Extract 1 calls her a 'self-abusive jazz genius' and Extract 2 talks of a life 'full of self-abuse'. The 'scandal and sensationalism' referred to in Extract 1 are foregrounded through alliteration, while Extract 2 draws attention to Holiday's private life by referring to '*sordid* details', which were 'chronicled in *lurid* books and *twisted* into soap opera'. (You may like to consider how different the meaning of the first part of this sentence would be if the emotive language were removed or changed: 'The Ø details of her private life chronicled in Ø books and *turned* into soap opera'.) What is also interesting is that Holiday's musical achievements and her private life are inextricably linked through the structure of the sentences:

Extract 1	Positive focus on her career	Linking section	Negative focus on her private life
	Holiday . . . finally received mainstream acknowledgement for achievements	often obscured by	scandal and sensationalism in her lifetime.
Extract 2	Negative focus on her private life	Linking section	Positive focus on her career
	The sordid details of her private life	have too often been allowed to obscure	the fact that . . . she managed to make an unforgettable art . . .

The way in which these two aspects of Holiday's life are linked in one sentence through the notion of one obscuring the other arguably has the effect of blending them in the reader's mind.

REPRESENTING IDEOLOGIES

So far, we have focused our attention on the way people are represented in texts, both as individuals and in groups. We now move on to consider the way texts represent ideologies – sets of values and beliefs which may be revealed explicitly through a text or through less direct strategies.

Language used in the public arena, be it spoken or written, can convey meanings which in some way reflect or consolidate the beliefs or values of a particular group. Much of the time, these public texts are the work of one speaker or writer, but they are appropriated by a group of people who see the text in question as an embodiment of what they stand for. However, sometimes a series of texts can work together to reinforce a particular ideology. For example, sermons, service books and hymns together construct a religious ideology, or what we might term a **discourse** of religion. (This is a different use of the term discourse from the one we used in Chapter 3.) Similarly, lessons, textbooks, essays and reports construct a discourse of education.

Exercise 3

The texts below are a selection of spoken and written observations about D-Day and about the commemoration of D-Day sixty years on. The D-Day assault took place in June 1944 when thousands of British, American and Canadian troops landed on the beaches of northern France in order to try to drive back the occupying German armies. The sixtieth anniversary of this event in June 2004 involved many war veterans returning to France and taking part in a service of remembrance.

Extracts (a) to (d) were all broadcast on 6 June, the day of the commemoration. The newspaper extracts (e) and (f) both appeared in print the following day.

What kind of ideology of the D-Day commemoration is constructed in these extracts? Focus your attention on:

- the attitudes of those who didn't fight towards the veterans
- the attitudes of the veterans to the anniversary
- the way the significance of D-Day is represented, both as an historical event and in terms of the sixtieth anniversary

Extract (a)

Sir Trevor McDonald is interviewing Colonel Derek Robbins, formerly of the Wiltshire Regiment, on ITV. They have just been talking about the allies reaching the concentration camps at the end of the war.

Key

TM	Sir Trevor McDonald
DR	Colonel Derek Robbins
(.)	micropause
(1.0)	longer pause, timed in seconds
[ ]	overlapping speech

	TM:	but those searing memories never leave you
	DR:	they don't leave you (.) no (.) they don't leave one (1.0) they are (.) grim (.) grim
5	TM:	so the sixtieth anniversary of D-Day is in many respects (.) in every respect (.) worth marking worth commemorating
	DR:	I couldn't agree with you more (1.0) it's er (1.0) and all the old soldiers are very grateful (.) to the way (.) the young and the country (.) have taken the trouble (1.0) to look after them in in er (.) Normandy and to help them in this anniversary
10	TM:	and what is also not forgotten (.) Colonel Robbins is that we (.) who are around today are all grateful to you (.) [DR: well] and to your (.) comrades
	DR:	very nice of you (.) of you to say that

Extract (b)

ITV's Mary Nightingale is interviewing Donald Sadler, a veteran of the Essex Yeomanry. They are at Gold beach, one of the three beaches on which British troops landed.

Key

MN Mary Nightingale
DS Donald Sadler
(.) micropause

	MN:	what are your thoughts Don when you come back (.) er er er today for an occasion like this what does it feel like to be here
	DS:	well it feels (.) it's a good feeling (.) you get a good feeling and you think you think about the lads who didn't come back you
5		know (.) and er (.) after all now it's sixty years ago now I came in forty-eight and I came in er I came in er eighty-eight and I came in ninety-four (.) eighty-four and ninety-four and this now two-o-o-four but um (.) it feels (.) great really and there's such a (.) lot of (.) the lads who are (.) who we know they all feel good you
10		know and it's a great feeling really

Extract (c)

ITV's Juliet Bremner is broadcasting from Ranville cemetery in Northern France.
Sir Trevor McDonald introduces her from Arromanches, on the Normandy coast.

Key
TM   Sir Trevor McDonald
JB   Juliet Bremner
(.)   micropause
(.h)   pause with intake of breath

	TM:	in a symbol of reconciliation this afternoon the German chancellor Gerhard Schröder will become the first German leader (.) to visit a British (.) war cemetery (.) Juliet Bremner is there in Ranville for us (.) Juliet (.) er there is some controversy to this visit isn't there
5	JB:	that's right (.) the little village of Ranville where I'm at the cemetery at the moment has decided that they would like to invite er Gerhard Schröder here this afternoon but it was not without its difficulties (.) he will be as you've just said (.) the first German head of state to come to any of these formal ceremonies (.h) it was so
10		sensitive to start with they decided to give up on the idea but they've decided now to go ahead with it and that's because the mayor of this village says (.) we must remember that times have changed (.) that now the Germans are very close allies close European friends (.) and that all the men who died during that
15		conflict whose graves you can see all around me (.) died more than half a century ago (.) and the world is a different place it's time to move on (.) even some Germans are saying that they see the D-Day invasion the D-Day landings as their liberation too

Extract (d)

This is an extract from the speech made by the Queen to the Normandy Veterans'
Association at Arromanches. The occasion is a large formal gathering and a parade
by the veterans.

	We are all getting older, and, while it is sad that this will be the final parade in Normandy of the Normandy Veterans' Association, it must not be forgotten that the members of the association continue to care for one another, to help each other in need, to support each other in loss, and
5	keep alive the memory of all that you achieved in those crucial days. The association can take great pride in all it has done and continues to do.

There is just one more thing I want to say. What for you is a haunting memory of danger and sacrifice one summer long ago, is for your country and for generations of your countrymen to come one of the proudest moments in our long national history. I take it upon myself to express the immense debt of gratitude we owe to you all. I salute you and thank you on behalf of our whole nation.

10

Extract (e)

This is the front page headline from the *Guardian* newspaper on Monday 7 June:

Sixty years on, D-Day veterans pass torch into hands of history

Extract (f)

This extract is taken from a report which appeared in the *Sun* newspaper on Monday 7 June:

The world yesterday paid its last major tribute to the glorious heroes of D-Day 60 years ago.

Thousands of survivors of the June 6 Normandy landings gathered for a series of moving, colourful and emotion-packed events.

For most of the veterans, now in their late 70s, 80s and some in their 90s, it was to be their final visit to the scene of the invasion that changed history.

The biggest amphibious assault ever seen, codenamed Operation Overlord, was commemorated on the beaches and drop zones where the troops landed – and in the cemeteries where many lie buried.

There was stringent security as 17 world leaders gathered to salute the men who fought to free Europe from Hitler's Nazi tyranny.

Suggestions for the answer can be found at the back of the book on p. 79.

SUMMARY

In this chapter we have seen that:

- Language is a representation of reality, not reality itself.
- Linguistic choices colour the representation of people, ideas, events, and so on.
- No two texts will represent the same thing in the same way.
- A collection of texts can work together to create an ideological discourse.

THEORETICAL APPROACHES   CHAPTER 7

In this chapter, we will be considering some of the theories about the interpretation of texts which have been influential in recent decades. These theoretical approaches are often complex and are embedded in the published work of a wide range of academics, so they will only be introduced here, where we will consider the essential ideas and approaches behind some of the theoretical positions.

In interpreting a text in a particular way or by using a particular approach, you may already have been adopting a theoretical position without being aware of it. Some of the theories which have been formulated have arisen from the work of linguists, while others have emerged as the result of work undertaken by literary critics. However, for our purposes, we can apply many of the approaches to both literary and non-literary texts. In fact, as was mentioned in Chapter 1, the division between literary and non-literary texts is no longer regarded as a clear-cut or necessarily useful one in terms of strategies for interpretation. Theoretical approaches have largely centred on the analysis of written texts, which is what we will concentrate on here, but there is no reason why you should not apply some of these approaches to spoken texts, if you think it appropriate.

THE ROLE OF THE READER

One significant shift in approaches to the interpretation of texts has been away from the author or originator of the text towards the reader or receiver of the text. This approach was a reaction to the traditional study of English literature when the student's main purpose in exploring a literary text was to try to identify what the author's intention was in writing it. The implication of this approach is that there could only possibly be one interpretation of a text – that which the author intended. Now, however, far more attention is given to the reader's role in constructing the text's meaning. The author, as pronounced by the French critic Roland Barthes (1925–80), is 'dead'. In other words, once the author has produced the text, they no longer have any input into its meaning and it is therefore up to the reader to form their own interpretation, which may or may not be the meaning the author intended. In fact, it could be argued that a text has no existence until it is, as it were, brought to life by a reader. A completed novel left in a drawer effectively has no existence until someone finds it and reads it.

With the shift on interpretation and meaning moving from originator to receiver, then the possibility of a text having many possible interpretations comes more fully into play. There are as many interpretations of a text as there are people who have read it (or heard it). A further point which was made by Barthes is that some texts require the reader's efforts to interpret them much more than others. In other words, there are some texts for which the majority of readers would concur on its meaning while there are others for which many different interpretations would be formulated. There is, if you like, a continuum of texts in terms of interpretative possibilities. Literary texts are often at one extreme of this continuum, and critics have often focused attention on those texts which are particularly likely to elicit multiple interpretations from their readers.

Exercise 1

The following extract is taken from the postscript (an additional chapter) of the professional cyclist Lance Armstrong's autobiography *It's Not About the Bike*, which was first published in 2000. The book focuses on Armstrong's fight against cancer and how he overcame this and fought his way back to health to win the 1999 Tour de France (an exceptionally long and gruelling race that lasts over three weeks). In the 2001 postscript he reviews his situation a year on, having won the Tour de France for a second time.

1. Read the extract carefully and consider whether you think this text is relatively transparent and therefore unlikely to allow multiple interpretations, or whether it makes demands on the reader which are likely to result in a multiplicity of interpretations.
2. Identify what it is about the way the text is written which helped you decide on your answer.
3. To what extent do you think the author's intention *can* be identified in reading this text?

How did the victory in 2000 compare with 1999? Physically, it was a harder race to win. As I sat there that night I was a very tired athlete. I think everybody in that race was relieved that it was over. Three weeks is an eternity for a sporting event, and when you finish, whether you finish
5 it in first place or in 101st place, it's a good feeling. It's a sense of accomplishment that changes a rider for the rest of their career.

There was a noticeable difference too, in the fact that the cancer wasn't the big story anymore – it was an item that was now mentioned on the second or third tier. I minded that. I wanted it to remain a topic of
10 conversation because it was important to get the message out. Since this book appeared, people have asked me what I mean when I say that given a choice between cancer and winning the Tour de France, I'd choose the

cancer. What I mean is that I couldn't have won even one Tour *without* my fight against cancer because of what it taught me. I truly believe that.

15 I had a deep sense of illness, and not only was I not ashamed of it, I valued it above everything.

Suggestions for answer

The text seems relatively straightforward to interpret. This is largely due to the fact it is an extract from an autobiography, the purpose of which is for the author to explain their own feelings and experiences to the reader. There would be no value to Lance Armstrong in not making it clear what he felt about his Tour de France wins and his cancer.

The first sentence of the extract is framed as a question. It is as if Armstrong is being interviewed, and his personal view being sought. Also, and inevitably for an autobiography, this is written in the first person so there is a strong sense of personal revelation. He often mentions his psychological condition, using vocabulary related to mental and emotional states, he notes that it was 'a good *feeling*' and he had 'a *sense* of accomplishment'. Similar vocabulary is used in the second paragraph when he goes on to talk about his cancer. He mentions how he 'minded' that it was no longer the main focus of interest in him and how he 'wanted' it to be discussed, and how he 'valued' his '*sense* of illness' above everything. The verb 'believe' and his statement that he was 'not ashamed' also reveal his feelings and attitudes.

It is hard to say whether the author's intention can be quite clearly identified in reading this text. Obviously he wants to write about two topics which are very important to him: his cycling and his illness. In line 12 Armstrong uses meta-language in response to an implied question by saying 'what I mean'. This suggests he is keen to make his view clear. In autobiographies, writers often make their purpose clear at the outset. However, this doesn't mean that Barthes's point about the author being dead is necessarily invalid: the reader still has to construct the meaning of the text, even though this particular one doesn't demand that the reader deliberate over different possible interpretations. Having said that, some readers may feel that Armstrong's intention is not primarily to explain his attitude to cycling and to cancer. Instead, they may feel he is more concerned to project a particular view of himself – either as a private person or as a celebrity. In that case, the 'I' of the text may be identified not with Armstrong the 'real' person, but with a projection or persona of Armstrong that he has created.

FOUR THEORETICAL APPROACHES

Exercise 2

By contrast with the extract above, some texts oblige the reader to think more consciously about what exactly the text might mean. As mentioned before, literary texts often lend themselves to multiple interpretations. Here is a poem written by the Victorian poet, Christina Rossetti.

1. Read the poem carefully, and then identify what it is about the poem which allows it to be interpreted in a variety of ways. How does the poem draw attention to the need for the reader to interpret its meaning?
2. Decide how you would interpret the poem's meaning.

My Dream

Hear now a curious dream I dreamed last night,
Each word whereof is weighed and sifted truth.

I stood beside *Euphrates** while it swelled
Like overflowing *Jordan** in its youth.
5   It waxed and coloured sensibly to sight;
Till out of myriad pregnant waves there welled
Young crocodiles, a gaunt blunt-featured crew,
Fresh hatched perhaps and daubed with birthday dew.
The rest if I should tell, I fear my friend,
10 My closest friend, would deem the facts untrue;
And therefore it were wisely left untold;
Yet if you will, why, hear it to the end.

Each crocodile was girt with massive gold
And polished stones that with their wearers grew:
15 But one there was who waxed beyond the rest,
Wore kinglier girdle and a kingly crown,
Whilst crowns and orbs and sceptres starred his breast.
All gleamed compact and green with scale on scale,
But special burnishment adorned his mail
20 And special terror weighed upon his frown;
His punier brethren quaked before his tail,
Broad as a rafter, potent as a flail.
So he grew lord and master of his kin:
But who shall tell the tale of all their woes?
25 An execrable appetite arose,
He battened on them, crunched, and sucked them in.
He knew no law, he feared no binding law,

*The rivers Euphrates and Jordan referred to in lines 3 and 4 are both mentioned in the Bible. The Euphrates was one of the rivers in the Garden of Eden; the river Jordan is the river in which Christ was baptized.

But ground them with inexorable jaw.
The luscious fat distilled upon his chin,
30 Exuded from his nostrils and his eyes,
While still like hungry death he fed his maw;
Till, every minor crocodile being dead
And buried too, himself gorged to the full,
He slept with breath oppressed and unstrung claw.

35 Oh marvel passing strange which next I saw!
In sleep he dwindled to the common size,
And all the empire faded from his coat.
Then from far off a winged vessel came,
Swift as a swallow, subtle as a flame:
40 I know not what it bore of freight or host,
But white it was as an avenging ghost.
It levelled strong Euphrates in its course;
Supreme yet weightless as an idle mote
It seemed to tame the waters without force
45 Till not a murmur swelled or billow beat.
Lo, as the purple shadow swept the sands,
The prudent crocodile rose on his feet,
And shed appropriate tears and rung his hands.

What can it mean? you ask. I answer not
50 For meaning, but myself must echo, What?
And tell it as I saw it on the spot.

Suggestions for answer

The poem can be interpreted in a variety of ways partly because it is 'unreal'. Crocodiles like these and the 'winged vessel' are clearly fictitious. At no point in the poem does the persona offer an interpretation of the dream. On the contrary, the persona several times asks the reader or addressee what they think the dream can mean. Many cultures view dreams as having some significance, so the fact that this tale is someone's dream draws our attention to the need for interpretation.

In deciding on your own interpretation of the poem, you possibly adopted a theoretical approach to the text without realizing it. The following section gives you some examples of other students' interpretations of 'My Dream' and explains two theoretical approaches associated with their interpretations.

Marxist readings

GD wrote: The crocodiles represent powerful nations and individuals, their wealth increasing with the magnitude of people in their state or the size of the state itself.

Caring for 'no law' the largest of the crocodiles devours the others, caring not for justice, but only for his own appetite. The poem could mean the dreamer believes that justice is not an inbuilt condition.

ML wrote: The eating of the smaller crocodiles could be representative of the Darwinian theory, which (it could be argued) we live by in modern society. So the stronger quashes the weaker . . . a take on the capitalist society maybe? The jewels on the crocodile hint towards greed and wealth.

EL wrote: I believe this poem is describing a city state and the effect corrupt or greedy politicians can have on it. The river at first, I believe, is the state itself: it 'waxed and coloured' representing the changes that take place there. The emergence of the crocodiles could be the introduction of those with unfair or unjust political ambition. They are the greedy or privileged. This is communicated through their 'gold / And polished stones'. The greatest is their leader, the most unjust or greedy who forces people to obey. The 'winged vessel' is justice, which brings about a resolution and restores the river to calmness.

These three students have all taken what is known as a **Marxist** approach in their interpretations. (Karl Marx was one of the key figures in formulating the political concept of communism.) One of the things which Marxist critics do is to focus on how texts (particularly literary ones) reveal issues of power and the struggle between social groups. Marxists often pay particular attention to how some texts (perhaps dangerously) reinforce the political or socio-economic status quo, or how they seek to undermine it. In this poem the students have identified the immoral status of those who oppress others for their own ends.

Psychoanalytic readings

JT wrote: I believe this poem to be about growth and regret, regret being born from the growth. The crocodile who wore a 'kinglier girdle', in his mission to become lord of the waters, killed all his brethren. Without thinking, he destroyed them all, but once he fell asleep, he went back to his normal size and 'all the empire faded from his coat'. This, to me, represents the fears and regrets that come to a mind before or during sleep, the fading of the empire symbolizing the truth that no matter how good a show you put on during the day of superiority and brilliance, at night, you cannot escape your self. The 'winged vessel' is, I believe, the crocodile's conscience.

CC wrote: My interpretation is that these two key images, the river and the crocodiles, represent a conscience. The first half of the poem portrays forgiveness and peace (through the biblical references to the Euphrates and the Jordan), therefore this represents the good side of the conscience. The image of the crocodile eating the others could therefore suggest the violent, bad thoughts that appear within the conscience.

FB wrote: The river represents purity, and out of the purity comes life – the crocodiles. The largest crocodile represents man, who acts with no restraint or fear of 'binding law'. The winged vessel represents religion which brings ideas of conscience and so remorse to man.

These three students have focused on what the poem could be saying about the mind, and about what motivates and controls human behaviour. They have taken an approach which might be used by **psychoanalytic** critics (influenced initially by the work of the psychologist Sigmund Freud) who explore the interplay, and often the tensions, between the conscious and unconscious mind, and how human beings develop a sense of self. They also look at how the sense of self is constructed – for better or worse – through the social context.

At the heart of many of the different approaches to texts which have been taken in recent decades is the idea that a text, rather like a picture, has some aspects which attract our immediate attention and others which seem to be more in the background. By shifting focus to the aspects of a text which are in the background, or even missing altogether, it becomes possible to formulate different interpretations of a text. In other words, by foregrounding aspects which at first seemed less important, we can change our perspective on a text's meaning. In addition, we have already seen how the context in which a text was composed can influence our interpretation of it, and this is an important aspect of some theoretical approaches. Other approaches put language and style at the forefront of interpretation.

Exercise 2 above gave some indication of a Marxist approach and a psychoanalytic approach to the interpretation of texts. Of course, some texts lend themselves more to the application of one theory than another. Two more theories are presented in Exercise 3 – feminism and structuralism. If you would like a fuller picture of the range of theories associated with modern approaches to texts, you may find Peter Barry's *Beginning Theory* (Manchester: Manchester University Press, 1995) of interest.

Exercise 3

This exercise is based on the opening of Jane Austen's 1813 novel, *Pride and Prejudice*.

1. Read it carefully and then briefly summarize what this extract seems to be about, first and foremost. How seriously do you think we should take these characters and their values?
2. Then shift your attention to the following aspects of the text:

   - the importance of marriage
   - the roles of men and of women
   - the way society works

It is a truth universally acknowledged, that a single man in possession of a good fortune, must be in want of a wife.

However little known the feelings or views of such a man may be on his first entering a neighbourhood, this truth is so well fixed in the minds
5 of the surrounding families, that he is considered as the rightful property of some one or other of their daughters.

'My dear Mr Bennet,' said his lady to him one day, 'have you heard that Netherfield Park is let at last?'

Mr Bennet replied that he had not.

10 'But it is,' returned she; 'for Mrs Long has just been here and she told me all about it.'

Mr Bennet made no answer.

'Do not you want to know who has taken it?' cried his wife impatiently.

'*You* want to tell me, and I have no objection to hearing it.'

15 'This was invitation enough.

'Why, my dear, you must know, Mrs Long says that Netherfield is taken by a young man of large fortune from the north of England; that he came down on Monday in a chaise and four to see the place, and was so much delighted with it that he agreed with Mr Morris immediately;
20 that he is to take possession before Michaelmas, and some of his servants are to be in the house by the end of next week.'

'What is his name?'

'Bingley.'

'Is he married or single?'

25 'Oh! single, my dear, to be sure! A single man of large fortune; four or five thousand a year. What a fine thing for our girls!'

'How so? how can it affect them?'

'My dear Mr Bennet,' replied his wife, ' how can you be so tiresome! You must know that I am thinking of his marrying one of them.'

30 'Is that his design in settling here?'

'Design! nonsense, how can you talk so! But it is very likely that he *may* fall in love with one of them, and therefore you must visit him as soon as he comes.'

'I see no occasion for that. You and the girls may go, or you may send
35 them by themselves, which perhaps will be still better, for as you are as handsome as any of them, Mr Bingley might like you the best of the party.'

'My dear, you flatter me. I certainly *have* had my share of beauty, but I do not pretend to be any thing extraordinary now. When a woman has
40 five grown up daughters, she ought to give over thinking of her own beauty.'

'In such cases, a woman has not often much beauty to think of.'

'But, my dear, you must indeed go and see Mr Bingley when he comes into the neighbourhood.'

45   'It is more than I engage for, I assure you.'

    'But consider your daughters. Only think what an establishment it
would be for one of them . . .'

Suggestions for answer

The extract is a conversation between Mr and Mrs Bennet. Mrs Bennet has discovered that an eligible bachelor, Mr Bingley, is moving into their neighbourhood
and is hoping he might prove a suitable husband for one of her five daughters. She
is urging Mr Bennet to call on Mr Bingley and introduce himself so that the rest
of the family can then become acquainted with him. The author uses gentle irony
to present this scene, laughing at the way Mrs Bennet assumes Mr Bingley is the
'property' of one of her daughters, and at the assumption (not at all 'universally
acknowledged' of course) that a single young man like him will be looking for a
wife.

The importance of marriage is indicated in the opening sentence but we realize that
it is presented primarily as something desired by women. The notion of being
married or being single is quickly established as a binary opposition, with marriage
as the 'norm' or the preferable state to being single.

The extract reveals a society in which men have more socio-economic power
than women. The daughters of a neighbourhood may well regard a single man as
their property but in fact marriage is more important to them for social and
economic security so they are almost obliged to look for an 'establishment' of that
kind. By contrast, Mr Bingley has financial independence, and he has the power to
choose a wife among the Bennet girls should he wish to do so. The roles of males
and females also differ in that social etiquette requires that Mr Bennet, the head
of the Bennet household, should really call on Mr Bingley first. The beauty of the
Bennet daughters seems to be an important consideration in attracting a husband.
By contrast, no attention is paid to whether Mr Bingley is physically attractive –
although quite a lot is made of his wealth. Youth is also connected with beauty.
Although Mr Bennet compliments his wife on her looks, she herself admits that
as a mother of five grown-up daughters, her own attractiveness is no longer
significant.

The society presented here seems very stable. This stability depends on marriage,
on social etiquette, and on a socio-economic structure where the wealth belongs
to privileged men like Mr Bingley, while others (who receive almost no attention)
are employed as servants.

Feminism

In exploring the role and presentation of women in the extract, particularly in the
way they contrasted with those of the men, the 'Suggestion for answer' was taking
a **feminist** approach to the text. Feminist critics have focused, among other things,

on the way women are represented in texts, particularly when they seem to be marginalized or disadvantaged in comparison to men. They also look at the way the presentation of males and females serves to construct or reinforce ideas about gender. In looking at this text, a feminist critic might ask whether Jane Austen's irony indicates that she herself is questioning the male and female roles and the attitudes associated with them, particularly in terms of marriage and female attractiveness. Feminist critics have paid a lot of attention to non-literary texts too.

Structuralism

You may also have noticed how much this extract is predicated on mutually exclusive pairs (the binary opposites we mentioned earlier). The male/female (which is implicitly heterosexual) and the married/single oppositions are particularly strong, but the young/old opposition is also present. These oppositions are strongly established through the language: for example in Mr Bennet's central question about Mr Bingley, 'Is he married or single?'. They establish for us the codes and values of the extract. This exploration of how one meaning is established through its relationship with another (through what it is not) is one of the approaches used by **structuralist** critics, for whom the analysis of how language creates meanings on various levels (from lexis to discourse) is central.

Finally, in looking at the way the society in this extract is represented, you may well have chosen to take a Marxist approach (as explained in Exercise 2), particularly if you focused on the economic principles present, and on a hierarchy in which servants are marginalized and the wealthy and privileged foregrounded.

Exercise 4

You may like to try applying some of these approaches to texts you are studying, or to texts used elsewhere in this book. Extracts which might prove particularly interesting are:

- Chapter 3, Exercise 1: *Winnie-the-Pooh*. Perhaps try a psychoanalytic reading or even a feminist one. You may like to look at some longer extracts from *Winnie-the-Pooh* too.
- Chapter 3, Exercise 3: 'The Princess and the Pea', the politically correct fairy story. Try any of the four approaches outlined.
- Chapter 6, Exercise 3: the D-Day texts. Try a feminist, Marxist or structuralist reading.

There are no suggestions for anwer to this exercise.

SUMMARY

In this chapter we have:

- considered the role of the reader in constructing and interpreting a text
- seen how some texts make more interpretative demands than others
- looked briefly at some of the theoretical approaches taken, namely Marxist, psychoanalytic, feminist and structuralist

SUGGESTIONS FOR ANSWER

CHAPTER 2, EXERCISE 4

In Sentence 1, the boy will, presumably, have been praised by a large number of people (such as members of the emergency services, members of the families involved and local people) and there is no need to mention precisely who they were. It is the schoolboy who is important, and our attention is focused on him as the subject of the sentence.

Although it is known who is responsible for the crisis in Sudan and for the displacement of so many people, in Sentence 2 this is less important than the fact that there are over a million people in desperate need of help. The repetition of 'people' in the noun phrases 'an estimated 1.2 million people' and 'many of these people' emphasizes where our attention should be focused.

Some people believe that the universe had a creator while others don't, so Bill Bryson has avoided this debate by making his sentences passive and not including an agent. Instead, the sentences are particularly effective in that the start of the universe is placed in the context of very short spans of time.

CHAPTER 5, EXERCISE 3

An interpretation of the poem

The poem is about an older woman and her feelings concerning love, memory and disappointment. Finding the sheet music, the widow is reminded of her youth, when she first sang or played the songs. Thinking of her youth is a pleasant experience as she recalls it being like a 'spring-woken tree' – an image of growth and promise. Love is often mentioned in the songs and she reflects on how as a young person she hoped love would bring her fulfilment. Looking back, however, she realizes tearfully that love had not brought her happiness and contentment in her youth, nor could it in her old age.

Some biographical detail about Philip Larkin

Andrew Motion explains in his biography of Larkin, *Philip Larkin: A Writer's Life* (London: Faber & Faber, 1993), that the poem was prompted by visits by Larkin to his mother and by his memories of his mother's songbooks. The biography also reveals Larkin as a man who longed for love and yet was equally afraid of being disappointed or constricted by love. (Larkin never married.) He did not view his own parents' marriage as a sound model for married life.

A possible re-interpretation

Motion implies that the poem says as much about Larkin himself as it does about his mother:

> the lessons Larkin draws from his mother's experience are the same as those he derives from his own. Love . . . might be able to redeem him from his unsatisfactory prime, but the terms on which he is prepared to let it exist are bound to limit its effects – if not crush them altogether.

In the light of the biographical information given, you need to consider whether you would reinterpret 'Love Songs in Age' as a displaced exploration of Larkin's own view of love, and his fears about expecting anything too positive from it.

CHAPTER 5, EXERCISE 4

Your impressions may have been similar to the following:

From the style of the writing, you may have noted that the writer seems very eloquent and well educated. In terms of what is important to the writer, love and forgiveness are central themes. The writer seems to have some reason to hate the addressee but has tried to go on feeling love. The writer comes across as noble, and as someone whose life has been ruined by the relationship with the addressee. According to the writer, the addressee is motivated by feelings such as hatred, vanity and greed. The addressee's actions seem to have ruined the writer, not deliberately but through being thoughtless. Clearly, the writer and addressee have had a close and intense relationship, and the writer feels love for the addressee. What cannot be deduced from the extract is the sex of the writer and the addressee. (You may have assumed it was a man writing to a woman, although the archery metaphor may challenge this notion.) The letter seems to have been written from a prison cell, and the writer has possibly committed a serious crime, judging by the reference to the 'terrible sentence'.

The actual circumstances:

The writer is Oscar Wilde (1854–1900) and he was writing to Lord Alfred Douglas ('Bosie'), with whom he had been in love for several years. He is writing to Bosie from Reading gaol, where he had been imprisoned following a conviction for homosexual acts. Ironically, Wilde's own trial and sentence were the result of his attempt to bring a libel case against Lord Alfred's father, an attempt which Lord Alfred had pushed Wilde to undertake.

Homosexual acts were illegal during Wilde's life, hence his imprisonment. Late Victorian attitudes meant that a man who had once been the toast of London for plays such as *The Importance of Being Earnest* and *Lady Windermere's Fan* was now ruined and his family disgraced. Wilde was sentenced to two years' hard labour and was forced to spend six hours a day walking a treadmill. The letter (of over 100 pages in the Penguin edition), which is titled *De Profundis* (*From the Depths*), is an extraordinary composition given the physical circumstances in which Wilde wrote it. He was only allowed one folded sheet of blue tissue paper at a time to write on and this meant he had no opportunity to check or revise his work. The intolerance of his age towards people of Wilde's sexual orientation makes the horror of his circumstances all the more poignant.

CHAPTER 6, EXERCISE 3

One of the most important attitudes expressed towards the veterans is that of gratitude for what they did (Extracts (a) and (d)). The *Sun*, (f), is very emotive in its praise for all the soldiers who took part in the D-Day landings, calling them 'glorious heroes' who freed Europe from tyranny. The Queen, (d), emphasizes the importance of the veterans' association, saying it should take '*great* pride' in its work. The veterans themselves express a positive attitude to the sixtieth-anniversary events, stating that it was worth commemorating, (a), and had given them a '*good* feeling', (b). The *Sun* again uses emotive language when it reports that the occasion was 'moving' and 'emotion-packed' for the returning survivors.

As an historical event, D-Day is represented as a very significant event: in the Queen's speech it is 'a *proud* moment' in the nation's history, while in the *Sun* it is an invasion that '*changed* history'. The occasion of the sixtieth anniversary enables a different perspective to be offered: in Extract (c), the commemoration is put in the context of times having changed and therefore reconciliation is possible. Even the defeated Germans can now see D-Day as part of their own 'liberation'. An interesting metaphor is used in Extract (e): the torch of remembrance is being passed into history. This implies that the time is coming when there will be no living survivors of D-Day, but the event will retain its historical significance. The metaphor of the torch, although quite commonly used to represent the continued importance of a cause or event, may also be regarded as an intertextual reference to John McCrae's poem which we examined at the start of Chapter 6.

GLOSSARY

This is a form of combined glossary and index. Listed below are the linguistic and literary terms used in the book, together with brief definitions, as well as key page references.

Active An active sentence is one in which the sentence subject is also the performer of the action referred to by the verb. (For example 'Raskolnikov murdered the old woman'.) (p. 17)

Addressee The person or persons at whom a text is directed. (p. 3)

Adjective A content word that normally has a descriptive function within a sentence. (p. 9)

Adverb A content word that typically gives information about how, when, where, or to what degree. (p. 2)

Agent In a sentence, the person or object carrying out the action of the verb. (p. 17)

Ambiguity When a word or expression has more than one possible interpretation or meaning. (p. 12)

Anaphor A linguistic element, usually a pronoun, that refers back to an item which has already been introduced, thus making anaphoric reference to that item. (p.21)

Anaphoric reference *See* 'anaphor'.

Auxiliary verbs A small group of function words made up of 'will', 'would', 'shall', 'should', 'can', 'could', 'may', 'might' and 'must'. (p. 10)

By-**phrase** A prepositional phrase beginning with 'by' that indicates the agent in a sentence. (p. 17)

Clause A unit of syntactic structure that typically contains an overt subject and always contains a verb element. (p. 20)

Cohesion The way in which the sentences in a text 'stick' together to form an orderly and integrated whole. (p. 19)

Collocation A combination of words that are habitually joined together such as in 'pull a pint'. (p. 5)

Conjunction A function word that has the property of joining elements together. (p. 10)

Content words Words that carry specific, easily definable meanings. Nouns, verbs, adjectives and adverbs are all content words. (p. 9)

Context The circumstances in which a text is produced or received, be they personal, literary, social or historical. (p. 43)

Definite article The determiner 'the', which is used to signify a specific noun. (p. 10)

Deictic words Words (such as 'today'/'tomorrow' or 'here'/'there') whose meanings are dependent on the context in which they are used. (The noun for this phenomenon is 'deixis'.) (p. 3)

Deixis *See* 'deictic words'.

Determiner A function word that appears only at the beginning of noun phrases. The most common determiners are the articles 'the' and 'a/an'. (p. 10)

Dialect A language variety that is distinct with regard to its lexis and grammar. For example, Standard English or the Cockney dialect. (p. 5)

Discourse (1) A stretch of language that makes up a complete unit or text. Discourse normally consists of one or more sentences, but a piece of discourse could be as short as a single noun such as 'exit'. (p. 19)

Discourse (2) The representation of something through the sum of several texts, for example, a discourse of religion. (p.60)

Discourse markers Language elements that perform the function of indicating the end of one section of discourse and/or the start of the next section. (p. 21)

Dysphemism A term that presents reality in a harsh way, and can be painful or uncomfortable in its directness. (p. 56)

Ellipsis The omission of a word or words that can be understood from the context. Ellipsis often results in informality. (p. 3)

Euphemism A term that presents reality in a gentler way, often in order to not hurt people's feelings and sensibilities. (p. 37)

Feminist criticism An approach to interpreting texts that foregrounds the representation of women. (p. 73)

Figurative language Language which is not literal but instead constructs meaning through metaphors, metonyms, similes and personification. (p. 25)

First person The pronouns 'I'/'me' and 'we'/'us' are first-person pronouns. A text is constructed in the first person if it is written from the point of view of 'I' or 'we'. (p. 4)

First person narrative A story told by one or more of the characters in the story, who will consequently use first person pronouns. (p. 5)

Function words Auxiliary verbs, conjunctions, determiners, prepositions and pronouns are all function words. Collectively, they make up a very small group of words. (p. 10)

Genre A particular type of discourse, such as a telephone message or a business letter. The adjective derived from 'genre' is 'generic'. (p. 35)

Indefinite article The determiner 'a' (or 'an'), which is used when the noun it accompanies does not have specific reference. (p. 10)

Intertextuality The relationships that exist between texts. (p. 31)

Lead paragraph In a newspaper report, the first paragraph, which has the function of giving the key information about the event reported. (p. 35)

Levels In this context, the various aspects of a text in which interpretation can take place, such as on a lexical level or a theoretical level. (p. 2)

Lexical cohesion Cohesion which is produced through the related meanings of words or through the repetition of a word in a piece of discourse. (p. 21)

Lexicon The full set of words in a language. (p. 13)

Lexis Vocabulary. The adjective is 'lexical'. (p. 9)

Literal language Language that employs no figurative strategies for meaning. (p. 25)

Marxist criticism An approach to interpreting texts which foregrounds issues of power and the relationships and struggle between social groups. (p. 70)

Metaphor A figurative use of language in which one thing is presented in terms of another with which it has some similarity. (p. 25)

Metonym A figurative use of language in which something or someone is referred to indirectly through a connected object. (p. 25)

Minor sentence A semantically complete unit, but one that is incomplete as far as clause elements are concerned and that typically lacks a verb element. (p. 16)

Narrative A story, or having the function of telling a story. (p. 22)

Non-standard grammatical features Any grammatical features which differ from the features of Standard English. (p. 5)

Noun A content word that has a naming function. (p. 9)

Noun phrase A word group that has a noun as its head word. (p. 2)

Onomatopoeia The mimicking of a sound by a word, although the representation is only approximate. The adjective is 'onomatopoeic'. (p. 22)

Parody A text that mocks or satirizes another text. (p. 36)

Passive A passive sentence is one in which the sentence subject is the person (or thing) on whom the action of the verb is carried out. (For example, 'The old woman was murdered by Raskolnikov.') (p. 17)

Persona The projected speaker in a text, as distinct from the author of the text. (p. 4)

Personification A figurative use of language in which a concept or something abstract, such as truth or air, is presented as a person. (p. 25)

Plagiarize To copy someone else's work and fail to acknowledge the true authorship. (p. 6)

Politeness marker Any linguistic item that is used by a speaker or writer to maintain a positive relationship with their audience. (p. 2)

Polysemy The fact of a word having more than one meaning. The adjective from 'polysemy' is 'polysemous'. (p. 11)

Preposition A function word that typically expresses the spatial (e.g., 'by', 'under', 'across'), temporal (e.g., 'after', 'during') or other (e.g., 'of', 'for') relationship between elements. (p. 10)

Present tense   One of the two tenses for which verbs can be marked in English, the other being the past tense. For example, 'I *walk*' is present tense, whereas 'I *walked*' is past tense. (p. 5)

Primary audience   The person or persons for whom a text is originally intended, be it spoken or written. (p. 49)

Pronoun   A function word, most typically a personal pronoun such as 'I', 'you', 'he', 'she', 'we' and 'they'. (p. 10)

Psychoanalytic criticism   An approach to interpreting texts that foregrounds the mind and what motivates human behaviour, particularly the interplay between the conscious and subconscious mind. (p. 71)

Recipient   The person for whom a text is intended. (p. 3)

Register   The style and level of formality of discourse that is the result of factors such as audience and purpose. (p. 22)

Representation   The way in which people and ideas (amongst other things) are presented in a text or texts. (p. 55)

Schema   A set format for constructing a text that is commonly recognized by users. (p. 3)

Second person   The second person pronoun is 'you'. The second person pronoun is used to address the listener or reader directly. (p. 5)

Secondary audience   Anyone hearing or reading a text who is not the primary audience for that text. (p. 49)

Semantic field   A theme or topic created by the occurrence of words with related meanings within a text. (p. 5)

Shared cultural knowledge   Knowledge about aspects of a social group that is shared by the majority of its members. (p. 5)

Simile   A figurative use of language in which one thing is compared to another using the prepositions 'like' or 'as'. (p. 25)

Standard English   The non-regional dialect used for public and educational purposes such as newspapers and textbooks, which is spoken by about 15 per cent of the British population. (p. 5)

Structuralist criticism   An approach to interpreting texts that foregrounds how meanings are created through one linguistic feature being juxtaposed with or opposed to another. (p. 74)

Subject   In sentence construction, the element that normally precedes the verb element. (p. 17)

Subordinate clause   A clause that cannot stand alone and is therefore subordinate to or dependent on some other element or part of the sentence. (p. 21)

Subordinating conjunction   A conjunction that introduces a subordinate clause and has the effect of making the clause subordinate. (p. 21)

Synonym   A word that has an identical meaning with another word, although arguably no two words are completely identical in this way. The adjective derived from 'synonym' is 'synonymous'. (p. 13)

Syntax   Word order. The adjective derived from 'syntax' is 'syntactic'. (p. 9)

Text   Any stretch of speech or writing that can be regarded as a complete unit, whatever its length. (p. 1)

Verb   A content word that refers to both actions and states and that can be identified by its ability to occur in present and past tenses. (p. 9)